3

S0-AIX-412

Music Editing for Motion Pictures

MUSIC EDITING

for

Motion Pictures

by MILTON LUSTIG

COMMUNICATION ARTS BOOKS

HASTINGS HOUSE, PUBLISHERS   New York 10016

ML
2075
.L 87

Copyright © 1980 by Milton Lustig.

All rights reserved. No part of this publication may be
reproduced, stored in a retrieval system, or transmitted,
in any form or by any means, electronic, mechanical,
photocopying, recording or otherwise, without the prior
permission of the copyright owner or the publishers.

Quoted and reproduced materials in this book, including photographs
specified on page 15, are the property of their owners and originators and are
used with their permission subject to the same reservation of rights above
stated. In particular, the name *Moviola* is a registered trade mark of the
Magnasync/Moviola Corporation.

Library of Congress Cataloging in Publication Data

Lustig, Milton.
    Music editing for motion pictures.

    Includes index.
    1. Moving-picture music. 2. Moving-pictures—
Editing. I. Title.
ML2075.L87   778.5'344   79-27002
ISBN 0-8038-4729-7

Published simultaneously in Canada by
Copp Clark Ltd., Toronto

Printed in the United States of America

To my family:
Anita, David, and Jill

Contents

Illustrations, Charts, and Tables

Preface

For many years I have sensed a need for a book on music editing. I couldn't leave the challenge alone. Some colleagues have advised me against writing it, feeling that there would not be enough calls for a book on this subject, but I have had to disagree with them since so much needs to be known and so many people need the knowledge of the subject.

This book has therefore been written to be understood and used by those with very little knowledge of music editing but with at least some knowledge of handling film. It should be immediately useful not only for potential music editors but also for composers and arrangers who are interested in motion-picture music. It should also be useful for those concerned with any area of motion-picture production; they must all interact with music editors and composers. Hence the book should help students and teachers in colleges and universities that have aspects of motion-picture production in their curricula—feature films, television films, training films, educational films—every kind of motion picture.

The music editor is the most important link between the film composer and the film for which he is to write the score. Composers are generally not fully familiar with all the technical operations that are needed in scoring for a film. These operations are in the expert field of the music editor; the composer needs to concentrate on creativity. Music editing is for the most part not highly creative though many of its phases benefit from a measure of creative insight. The music editor's work is a service needed by the composer of motion-picture music and by many others. The explanations in this book should demonstrate these needs.

Motion pictures with music *have* been done without the services of a music editor. Motion pictures with music *have* also been done without the services of a composer—by a music editor working alone. But even if one of them can be dispensed with, together they can accomplish better work. In any event, someone must perform each function.

Some composers sit at a film editing machine and do all their own timings and preparation. Many composers like to do this work; some must do it when they are scoring a very low-budget film whose producer may not even know what a music editor is and could not afford one anyhow. The finished score still needs a person with film know-how, whatever his title and even if he is not a music editor, to cut and assemble the final product for dubbing. When this person is not a music editor, the composer is needed to stand by and help or even supervise.

I have always felt that being a musician should be a prerequisite for music editing. However, I know personally some very fine music editors who are not musicians and who have had no musical training. They have worked in their profession for so many years that they couldn't avoid absorbing a great deal of musical knowledge, at least enough for doing what is required of them, such as the ability to follow a music score.

I have tried to present everything about music editing that a book can offer, plus additional information and charts that will be of value even though they are not everyday needs. In more than forty years of being engaged in my profession, I believe that I have come upon just about every type of problem imaginable. Some of these have been real beauties but none have been impossible to solve—some just took longer. For these and for routine problems, this book may give some future colleague at least a small head start.

Milton Lustig

Sources and Acknowledgments

Colleagues and friends kindly allowed me to show photographs of their work and equipment:

Glen Glenn Sound: The Dubbing Log
Hollywood Film Company: The Synchronizer
KEM Editing Systems: The KEM
Bruce Knudson: The page from *Project Tempo,* The Click Track Book, by Carroll Knudson
Magnasync/Moviola Corporation: The Moviola
United Recording Electronics Industries (UREI): The Digital Metronome
Veeder-Root: The Veeder-Root Counters

The technical illustrations were prepared by Jack Neville.
The photographs are by David Lustig.
My associates Bill Vogt and Dick Ryan of Glen Glenn Sound furnished me valuable assistance regarding electronic information, for which I gladly thank them.
The manuscript was prepared for publication by Willis L. Parker.

M. L.

Music Editing for Motion Pictures

1 / **The Spotting Session**

You are now on the assignment as music editor for a film. You are ready for the first and one of the most important phases of the work, the spotting of the film for its music. "Spotting" is the word generally used for the making of decisions about the music—where it will start and where it will end. It is usually done in a session when the picture is run in a special projection room that is equipped to run it forward and reverse, with stops inbetween. The director, the producer, the composer, and many others take part in the session. As the picture is being run reel by reel, spots are cued for the music and you as the music editor will be giving each cue a number. The sequences being considered for music may be run back and forth many times. This is normal.

Numbering Cues

There are many systems for numbering cues. Some music editors or composers like to number the cues 1M1 for the first cue in reel 1, 1M2 for the second cue in reel 1, 1M3 for the third, and so on. Some like to use M11, M12, and M13. Some use M101, M102, and M103. Take your choice. You may even need to use Reel 1, Part 1, and so on that way. When a cue starts in one reel and continues in the next, the cue numbers must indicate the fact. For example, if the fourth cue in reel 5 continues into reel 6, the cue would be called M54/61 or 5M4/6M1 or M504/601—or even Reel 5 Part 4, Reel 6 Part 1.

Keeping the Record

In addition to numbering cues, you may also be making all the notes during this screening and indicating any pertinent remarks made by the composer or the producer or whoever has the word of authority. The producer may tell the composer something like, "See if you can give me a little suspense feeling on the cut to so and so." Or: "Don't overemphasize his funny walk." Though he is talking to the composer, you had better be making notes about these remarks. Since this session is the all-important first step in scoring the picture, everything that is said here helps the composer. You as the music editor may be the *only* person writing any notes at all, so remembering all the information that comes out of this spotting session depends on you. You might also be asked to contribute some worthwhile suggestions of your own as the spotting continues on. But not always—I have worked on pictures where no one has asked my opinion and it has even been suggested that I offer no suggestions at all because the other people will make all the decisions. In contrast, I have been on spotting sessions where the others felt my knowledge was better than theirs and they practically wanted me to spot the whole picture for music cues. Some composers who were relatively inexperienced or new in the business have said: "Don't be afraid to speak up. I'm sure that you have more experience along these lines than I have." Sessions like these always make for a great relationship from the very beginning and you can't help really striving to contribute when your creative ability has been called upon.

The spotting session can run as short as a few hours or it may take days, depending on how many times the sequences under consideration are run back and forth, or how uncertain those present may be as to what they really want. It may take many runnings in a particular area to come to a final decision just where to start. The session may run very smoothly and then some sequence can produce such a hassle that it takes forever to come to any decision.

As an added precaution to make sure you haven't missed anything that was said at the spotting session, or in case you wish to verify what you wrote, it's a good idea to have a cassette recorder running throughout the session. This precaution, of course, would be most needed when the spotting is done in a projection room. On the cassette tape you would not only hear the voices of those in the room but also the dialogue from the screen. The best demonstration of why I think the cassette recorder method is so good happened when a director once said: "Music in after that line." He was a bit impatient and didn't give too much consideration to my writing speed. I didn't get the chance to write down which line the music was to come in after. The film continued on but I didn't need to say anything; I knew that when the cassette would be run, I would hear the line he was referring to and would get the information on the line of dialogue from that.

Equipment

I have done many spotting sessions on a Moviola® because a projection room was not available at the time. The Moviola is a machine designed to show the picture and play the sound track. It is the one indispensable piece of equipment used by picture editors, sound-effects editors, and music editors—all of them. On the Moviola, the picture can be run and synchronized with one or more sound tracks. It has two counters, one reading the time as footage, in feet and frames, the other (which music editors use especially) reading the time in seconds and tenths of seconds. Some projection rooms are equipped with footage counters, which help very much.

In recent years a different piece of equipment has been introduced that is becoming more popular with many picture editors. These machines are called flatbeds. They are very impractical for the actual editing operations of sound-effects or music editors, as they have many drawbacks for both types of work, but picture editors and directors love them and they are excellent for spotting sessions. They have the advantages of a large screen, high speeds for both forward and reverse, and much quieter operation than Moviolas. They are also more expensive.

I have found it preferable to spot the picture on either of these machines rather than in a projection room. The reason I prefer them for this work is that I can do another important part of my work at the same time as the spotting of the music. If the spotting is done in a projection room, it is then necessary to run the entire picture again on the Moviola, in order to do all the markings and measurements of the cues before starting to do any individual timings. A Moviola or

Moviola® with Double Sound Head

flatbed allows you to mark the exact starting frame of each cue with a grease pencil on the film; you could not do this in a projection room, obviously. You can also measure the overall length of each cue in minutes and seconds, and you can measure how far down in the reel each cue will start.

KEM Flatbed

The latter measurement is in footage and frames, measured from the *start mark* at the head of each reel. Each reel will start at zero (0000) on the Moviola's footage counter. You zero the counter after threading up the film on the machine with the start mark in the aperture. (This is the opening on the Moviola or flatbed where the frame is in viewing position). The counter will run cumulatively with the film. It is then a simple matter to note that cue 7M3, for instance, starts on 574 feet and 6 frames in the reel. On the footage counter there are five discs. The first four run like those in any other counting machine, counting whole feet. The fifth counts frames; it is marked off into 16 segments for the 16 frames in each foot. One complete revolution of this last disc and the adjacent one goes to the next number.

The following diagram shows the seconds counter and the footage counter. The footage counter is showing how the 574 feet plus 6 frames looks.

The seconds counter is geared to give its reading in cumulative seconds; it does not convert them to read in minutes. When the counter reaches 60 seconds it does not turn over to read 1:00. It continues on and therefore 1 minute + 1 second will read not as 1:01 but as 61 seconds. This really presents no problem at all. You can reset the counter to 0000 each time it reaches 60 seconds and then just

Seconds and Footage Counters

keep track of the minutes as you go. This is common practice and, especially while timing, it isn't likely that you can get confused. You are timing with such small fractions of each second that you automatically know where you are all the time. The last disc on the seconds counter reads in tenths of a second.

The seconds counter and the footage counter are geared to move simultaneously. When the seconds counter turns over 1 second, the footage counter turns over 1 foot plus 8 frames, that is, 24 frames. You usually reset the seconds counter to read zero for the beginning of each music cue, but you do not reset the footage counter until you zero it for the beginning of a new reel.

The Book Work

From the time of the spotting session, the composer is very anxious to have the breakdown as soon as possible. Rather than have him wait until the timings are done, the breakdown should be completed before starting the individual timings.

The composer will be using this breakdown to total the minutes and seconds of what he must write, how much of it will be scoring and how much will be source music. (Source music and scoring are de-

THE BAD NEWS BEARS IN BREAKING TRAINING

#10965

MUSIC BREAKDOWN   June 16th 1977

REEL ONE

M 11   Main Title information not yet available   30+0

M 12   On cut to coach's feet walking towards kids   240+15
0:22.4
                Out on his dialogue to the kids: "Look
                alive gentlemen."

M 13   On kids reacting to Kelly coming on cycle.   549+4
1:42.1
                SEGUE on cut to Lupus in bed.

M 14   SEGUE on cut to Lupus in bed.   702+6
1.17.7
                Out at end of reel.

REEL TWO

M 21   Starts 1½ seconds after cut to coach   572+8
1:52.2   waving to the parents as they leave.

                Out on cut to Fatty looking out the rear
                window.

REEL THREE

M 31   On cut to Kelly driving as seen thru the   23+6
1:06.6   windshield.   THIS WILL BE A SONG

                Out on night scene of motel

M 32   SOURCE for interior of liquor store.   383+4
0:31   In progress.

                Out on cutaway, in progress.

The First Page of a Music Breakdown

fined in Chapter 2.) He will also plan the number and length of recording sessions he will need and the size of the orchestra for each session. As an example, he may feel that one scoring session with a large orchestra will handle the cues for which it is necessary. Then perhaps one other session will suffice to do the cues that need only a smaller orchestra. A session of source music cues may then be done with a small group, perhaps five or six musicians.

Page 25 shows a sample first page of a spotting-session breakdown. Copies of the breakdown go to all who attended the session and also to anyone else who may have need of a copy. The picture editor will get one. He can then know if any of your timings are affected should he have to make any changes within the duration of any music cues after the timings have been done; and he can then let *you* know. The breakdown is also very useful to the sound-effects editor. It gives him a guide as to whether he has any musical support in a sequence for which he is doing sound effects. Sound-effects editors have called and asked: "Is there any music going on here? I'm not so sure that what I've done will carry it by itself."

It will be noted on the sample page that M11, the Main Title, has not yet been established at the time of the spotting session. At this stage of operations this postponement is very common. The titles are usually the last things to be done so you should list the cue as shown: "not yet available."

In making the breakdown, I prefer to put the timing of the cue under the cue number. At the right side of the page put the footage and the frame where the cue starts in the reel. Remember that these points are only suggestions and you may do anything to make your book work most convenient for you.

After the spotting session is over, the breakdown notes can be typed. Getting them typed concludes the first phase of the music editor's assignment.

2 / Source Music and Scoring

All music in films is either source music or scoring. The source music is so called because it supposedly emanates from within the picture itself, such as a person listening to a radio, a juke box playing, or music in a restaurant even though you never see the musicians. In other words, the performers in the picture hear this music as well as the audience. All these examples are nonvisual source music. If the audience sees an entertainer perform, someone singing a song, or a marching street band, this is visual source music. Scoring, on the other hand, is the background music that is written for the picture by the composer and is never heard by the characters in the film, only by the audience. Some refer to scoring and source music as "ours and theirs." The distinction is very well worded.

Sometimes a composer can skillfully blend the two. I remember a picture where a man was sitting in his yard, playing a cello all alone. After a while the camera started to pan away and suddenly another instrument started to play a counterpoint to his solo. A moment later, more instruments entered. The cello eventually disappeared and before you knew it, what started out as a source cue turned into a scoring cue without the audience being aware. This blending is not often done, but was extremely effective in this case.

3 / **The Stopwatch**

A stopwatch is very important for the music editor to have. He may use it at the spotting session, on the scoring stage, or on the set. It does a lot more than just tell the elapsed time of an action. It is also used for determining the click tempo of a piece of music or a visual action. If you want to determine the tempo of a piece of music, you would start your watch on the count of one second and stop it on the count of twenty-five seconds. This series then has twenty-four intervals. (The count of two is at the end of the first interval.) If you read the seconds on the watch as a tempo rather than as seconds, they will give you the click frame beat you were timing. The number you are looking at tells you the number of frames per beat. All tempos in music editing are referred to this way. This click frame beat is not to be confused with the metronome beat, which marks beats per minute and has nothing to do with click tempos.

There are stopwatches that have three scales: seconds, 16mm footage, and 35mm footage. The click tempo can also be determined on either of the two footage scales.

To determine the beat on the 35mm footage scale you would start on one and stop on seventeen. Reading the footage would tell you the tempo just as in reading the seconds when counting to twenty-five. To determine the beat on the 16mm scale you would start on one and stop on forty-one.

The reasoning for all this is simple mathematics. You use twenty-four intervals on the seconds scale because there are twenty-four frames per second. You use sixteen intervals on the 35mm scale because there are sixteen 35mm frames to the foot. You use forty intervals on the 16mm scale because there are forty 16mm frames to the foot.

If you want to get the tempo of something that doesn't run long enough to count to seventeen, twenty-five, or forty-one (whichever scale you are using), then just continue counting even though the action or the music has stopped. If a person walked only five steps you would just count without the picture and try to maintain your tempo.

4 / Timing on the Moviola

The spotting session is over and the composer is patiently waiting for you to start giving him the timing sheets. Each timing is for an individually timed cue that you will set up to start at zero (0000.0) on the seconds counter and will time until the point where the music is to go out. The composer cannot do very much without these timings but he may be busy developing themes in the meantime. He has the breakdown notes from the spotting session and these give him quite a lead. He can plan his orchestra setup, as was mentioned, hence has something to work on while you are working on the timings.

Synchronizing the Track and Picture

To get perfect synchronization, you must thread up the sound track on the Moviola in an exact relationship to the picture. Standard procedure is to thread the picture on its start mark and then to thread the sound track on *its* start mark. For normal running purposes, this procedure is accurate enough, but when you work with critical synchronization, more accuracy than this is required. Just arbitrarily putting the start marks on each head is not enough.

Why not? In consequence of the intermittent movement of the picture film, the frame is motionless for about three-quarters of the twenty-fourth of a second allowed for each frame. The other quarter of that twenty-fourth of a second is used for transporting the film to the following frame. You can turn the picture flange (situated to the left of the picture head) and the picture will not move if you caught it in the right place, *but the sound will;* the sound is always in motion and moves smoothly. While the frame is motionless, therefore, you have to choose one of three sprocket holes in which to place your sound start mark in the sound aperture. You can never know when your choice is correct in this "standard" procedure.

To place the sound track properly, have the frame line of the picture in the middle of the picture aperture on its way up to viewing position. Now set the top of the frame line of the sound start mark in the center of the sound head. You are now in perfect synchronization.

Writing the Timing Sheets

Timing is, at best, a boring part of your assignment but it is an extremely important function because everything the composer writes comes from the information you give him. What you are really doing is telling the story of each cue beginning on zero where the music starts, and progressively telling everything that happens throughout the cue. You give the timings in seconds and tenths of a second of each action as indicated on the seconds counter. Although you have zeroed the counter at the start of each cue, your footage counter is undisturbed. You set this only once at the head of the reel.

Undoubtedly the composer will never use more than 10 percent of the actions you will be timing. Yet you must time them all, because you would generally have no way of knowing which actions he is going to incorporate into his writing and he probably doesn't know either at this time. This is why you must take down the timings of everything you see and of everything you hear on the sound track. This record will not be merely for timing purposes; it provides continuity of story in explicit detail. One full typewritten sheet of this detail may have about one minute of timing on it but it is not unusual to fill about two sheets for a minute of timings, especially if a lot of fast action is going on in the scene.

Taking down the dialogue from the sound track does have a tendency to slow up your speed as compared to just taking down visual action. When timing dialogue, for one comparison, you should indicate exactly what is said. Do not refer to it by saying: "She asks him what he's doing in the evening." This does not contain a quotation of

| 0:51.3 | Cut back to her as she continues: "If you can't be |
| 0:55.5 | an athlete be an athletic supporter." |

0:56.1   She shows a slight reaction to what she thinks she heard herself say.

0:56.6   Cut to a classroom door as Sandy is hurriedly coming thru.

| 0:56.9 | Voice continues: "Now for some major economics." |
| 0:58.6 | |

0:58.8   Door slams when Sandy enters.

0:59.2   Cut to the classroom and the teacher

0:59.8   They all look up at her as voice continues: "School lunches have been promoted - -

1:01.7   Cut to reverse angle of everyone looking at Sandy. She is embarrassed. Voice continues - -from twenty five cents - - -

1:03   She walks towards the teacher. Voice continues - - to thirty five cents. - -Sorry kids. Yearbook pictures have gone - -

1:07.4   Cut to a C.U. of her friend trying to whisper to her as voice continues: - - to two fifty a set - -

1:08.7   Cut to Sandy looking at her. Voice: - -and senior rings - -

1:10.2   Sandy hands note to teacher. Voice: - -from twenty five - -

1:10.6   Cut to teacher as she is handing him note. Voice: - -to thirty five dollars."

1:13.1   Teacher reads note. Voice: "Several of - -

1:13.6   Cut to Sandy looking at him. Voice - - -last years seniors - -

1:15.4   She starts to walk away. Voice: - -have been offering cut rate - -

1:17   Cut to Danny bringing in a jar with frogs. Voice - - buys on their used rings - -

A Timing Sheet: *Grease*

the dialogue. The proper way is to indicate the actual dialogue and write:

```
She says: "By the way, what are you doing tonight?"
```

Sometimes it is difficult to take down a long dialogue sequence when it is interrupted with various actions and scene cuts while the dialogue is going on. This type of timing is illustrated on the timing sheet from the picture *Grease,* Cue M21 page 3. Notice how it is written and how the underlining helps make the dialogue readable even though it is disjointed.

Never backtrack with the numbers. Do not do anything like this:

```
1:47      Sally says: "Why don't you just tell him
1:50.5    that you don't care to go there again?"

1:49      She puts the glass on the table.
```

The single spacing of 1:50.5 after the 1:47 is just one way of indicating the end of the dialogue. All other timings are always double spaced. But notice the bad continuity of the numbers. It can seem like a mistake. Show the timing this way:

```
1:47      Sally says: "Why don't you just tell him that -

1:49      She puts the glass on the table as she continues:
1:50.5    - - you don't care to go there again?"
```

In this form the timings are going consecutively.

Try to describe as best as you can what the action is. Write with descriptions such as these:

```
Cut to a closeup of him with guilt written all over
his face.
```

or:

```
He looked like he had walked for hours in the rain.
```

Writing in this manner is of great help to the composer in creating the mood. It refreshes his memory of what he has seen at the spotting session. You must also remember that many times the composer may not have the opportunity to again view the picture you are describing until he arrives on the scoring stage, so you can see the importance of your work. He may not see the picture even on the scoring stage, since not all scoring is done with projection of the picture on the screen. Much of it is done with click tracks only. (A complete explanation of clicks and how they are used is in Chapter 5.)

The Composer's Needs

There are numerous ways for composers to work when scoring a film. Some will be provided with a duplicate copy of the picture and sound track and will work at home with a Moviola. A duplicate or dupe picture is just a black and white print of the original color, and is used strictly for work purposes. Dupes of the picture and the work track are usually made for the sound-effects and music editors after the final picture editing. Since both departments are usually working at the same time, copies for each become necessary. If the color were used, it would be receiving rather rough treatment due to its numerous splices. In addition, the picture editor may be reviewing it continually for improvements which he would subsequently correct in the dupes. Dupes are splice-free.

Some composers like to work with a videocassette copy of the film. It is certainly very convenient and takes up a lot less space than a Moviola. When the picture is transferred to a videocassette, a time code that shows on the screen is usually added to it. The time code is in a series of numbers that can be superimposed on the picture in almost any position and in any size that may be desired. It can serve various purposes. For one, it prevents unlawful duplication of the film. The code shows four sets of numbers in a horizontal line with separations between the sets. The first set is the reel number. The second set reads in minutes. The third set reads in seconds. The fourth set reads in videoframes per second, which is 30. There is no direct comparison between this and film frames so it is best to ignore this last figure. The time code's printed timings in no way conform to your music timings. They run continuously from the beginning of the reel to the end and should only be used by the composer for arbitrary timings between points. The exact timings he will get from your timing sheets.

Some composers will also rent a flatbed occasionally. Whatever method they use, they do like the idea of viewing the picture as much as possible.

CUE ____ M71A-M71B   SCORING START __210+0____

TITLE ____ THE HILTON _____ CLICK TEMPO 16/2 and 9/6

STARTS AT __228+10__ IN REEL   WARNING CLICKS __8 free__

DATE __ June 10, 1977 __

REVISED 6/14/77

        Mike and Orlansky walk up to the kids after walking away from Morrie on the field. Mike says to Tanner: "Tanner, give Mr. Orlansky a fresh beer." After the kid gives it to him Orlansky says: "What would ya say if I told ya Anheuser Busch is gonna put ya all up personally?"

7/A (0:00) MUSIC IN a beat after his line as we cut to the kids cheering. They run to surround him.
16/2

CLICK 0:04.4 Cut to a closer shot of Orlansky getting mobbed by the kids.

0:07.1 Cut to later. They are riding into town by car.

0:12.9 Kelly jumps out before car comes to a full stop.

7/B (0:14.2) He starts to run

22ND 0:14.6 Cut to car fully stopped as kids get out.

CLICK AND
START OF 0:18 Cut to elevator door opening. Kids come running out and down the halls.
9/6

0:26.7 First kid makes a run for the first room. From here on it looks like a game with the kids running in and out of the different rooms.

0:35.8 One kid who runs in from the foreground pauses.

0:37.2 Starts to run back.

0:40.6 Two kids meet in the hall and slap hands. Then they start to congregate and talk about their rooms.

0:48.2 They all start to run into another room after one kid yells something to them. It is difficult to tell what they are saying.

0:51.3 Cut to a kid running into Kelly's room.

A Timing Sheet: *The Bad News Bears.* Note the REVISED date, the prologue, the 0:00 timing entry, and the margin additions.

It is necessary to start your timing sheets with a short prologue describing the action before the music cue starts. Your 0:00 should *not* be the first thing the composer reads on the timing sheet. He should be refreshed as to what the action was prior to the start of the music. A sample of this kind of prologue is illustrated on the timing sheet of *The Bad News Bears.* You can see how reading this prologue helps put a composer into the proper mood to start his work.

There are times when a prologue is not necessary at all. If the cue you are about to time has segued from the end of another cue, it is understandable that the entire previous cue has become the prologue and consequently you can start timing with 0:00 immediately. To segue (pronounced *seg-way*) means to go from one piece of music to another with no pause. If you are going to time cue 3M6 that segued from cue 3M5, you would start it as follows:

    0:00   SEGUE from the end of cue 3M5 at 1:24.6

The last line of cue 3M5 would read:

    1:24.6 SEGUE to 0:00 of cue 3M6

All cuts must be indicated also. Look again at the sample timing of *The Bad News Bears.* At 0:26.7 the way the action is described should make a very clear picture of what is happening.

At the conclusion of the timing, as a reference, always go a bit further than the actual end. The composer may want to know what happens after he reaches the point where the music is to end as originally planned in the spotting session. He might feel he'd like to carry the music a bit further. In a hypothetical example, the end of a cue could read as follows:

    1:16.7   MUSIC OUT as he sits down.

             Reference:
             1:17.3   Cut to Linda looking at him.

             1:17.8   She says: "I thought that would
                      surprise you."

             1:20.9   Cut to him saying: "I'm not
             1:22.3   surprised at all."

Indent the reference timings after indicating the MUSIC OUT just for simplicity and to show that it is strictly a reference. This reference gives the composer the option to continue on if he wishes.

Notice also, on the timing sheet from *Grease,* that at the end of a line of dialogue, the end timing is *single spaced* to show that this is where it ends. You will see this at 0:55.5 and again at 0:58.6. Notice that at 0:59.8 there is no single-spaced timing. This means that the dialogue is continuing on the very next line and there is no pause.

There are other good methods of indicating dialogue timings which you may like better. There are no hard and fast rules. I have seen timings where the music editor puts the start of dialogue timing in the usual place and puts the end timing in a far right column as follows:

0:51.3   Cut back to her as she continues: "If   0:55.5
           you can't be an athlete, be an athletic
           supporter."

There are editors who take a separate line to indicate the end of dialogue. They write EOL, meaning "end of line," as follows:

    0:51.3   Cut back to her as she continues: "If
               you can't be an athlete, be an athletic
               supporter."

    0:55.5   EOL

Cues between Reels

In timing a cue that starts in one reel and continues in the following reel, the timing is continuous as though it were in one reel. How this is handled for the scoring stage will be discussed later in Chapter 22, Preparation for Scoring. The simplest way to keep the seconds counter in continuity when changing reels on the Moviola is as follows:

When you reach the last frame of picture on the reel, go to the first frame of end leader which is the very next frame. *Do not touch* your seconds counter but reset your footage counter to 0000 at this frame. You can now remove the outgoing reel from the Moviola. Now back up to 9988+0 on the footage counter with *no film* on the Moviola. This is 12 feet back from 0000. Your seconds counter, from which you are reading your timings, will also be going back exactly 12 feet, which is 8 seconds. Reset your footage counter to 0000. Again, *do not touch the seconds counter.* Set up your next reel with the start mark on this 0000. When you go forward and reach the 12-foot reading on the footage counter it will be the first frame of this new reel. Your seconds counter will be where it was when you removed the outgoing reel. Your reading of seconds will be uninterrupted. You can now continue your timings. This procedure should be followed whether the timing is from an A to a B reel or a B to an A reel. (All odd-numbered reels are A reels and all even-numbered reels are B reels.) The only difference when timing goes from a B reel to an A reel is that it should be brought to the attention of the composer on the timing sheet because this is a projection-machine changeover. For theatrical release, all A reels are joined to the following B reels to make 2000-foot reels. For all studio work however, all reels are 1000 feet long maximum. They become 2000-foot reels only when release prints are made. The longer reels would be far too clumsy to work with.

When the timing goes from a B reel to an A reel, the composer should be aware of how to write for this situation. The music in the outgoing reel should end at the end of the reel. There should be a pause of at least two-thirds of a second before continuing in the next reel. Certainly there should be no music sustaining over this point, in order to avoid a bump caused by the projection crossover. This precaution does not mean that the music must come to an end in the outgoing reel. It means that the music should be so designed by the composer as to accommodate what must take place mechnically. If properly planned the transition will work beautifully. Most composers know how to write when this need occurs, but it is a good habit for the music editor to remind them on the timing sheet.

There should be a sheet for every cue in the picture, even if there is nothing for the composer to do. If 7M5, for instance, were a playback or a production track that didn't require anything from the composer, a sheet with that indication should be sent to him so he can keep his book in order and will know that nothing is missing and that you haven't forgotten to send him a timing.

Timings for Source Cues

When giving timings for source cues, it is usually not necessary to time with the completeness of a scoring cue. Generally an overall length will suffice, because this source music will be cut in to cover the scene and almost any position of this music will be acceptable. If it were necessary to play source music over a scene in a restaurant that runs about 2 minutes in the picture, I would indicate on the timing sheet that I need about 2½ minutes of restaurant music. The reason for having it longer is for protection in case you should need to play around with its position because something in the music didn't work well with something in the picture. As an example: There is a restaurant scene that is about 1:35 in length. If the composer were to write exactly 1:35 of source music, it would have to be used just as it is. But suppose a passage in the music was a bit too loud and had a tendency to interfere with dialogue at that particular point; then you couldn't shift the position of the exactly 1:35 source music. If you moved its position you would be short either at the beginning or the finish and overlength at the opposite end. But if the cue were at least 2 minutes long, you would have the option of sliding the music to a much better placement and would still have enough at both ends.

There is also the possibility that the picture editor might decide to lengthen the restaurant scene; recording overlength is good insurance against this.

Once in a while a composer may want a little more information than just an overall timing. You may be asked to semi-time source cues. The composer wants to know at what timings some of the important actions happened and where the dialogue started and stopped. He doesn't care to know exactly what they were talking about, only to have a reference. In regular timing of scoring music, the dialogue should be exact. In the case of source music, exact timing really is not necessary. The composer and you would discuss this special need. He doesn't want you to do any more work than necessary when he knows he isn't going to use it.

Language Problems

My most recent assignment confronted me with an unusual situation in working with a composer. He spoke only Italian. Communications had to be a problem. To solve it, everything was timed in the usual manner but the composer was not given the original timing sheets. Instead, after each cue was timed, I reproduced a copy of the sheet but masked off all the action continuity; only the heading and the timings down the left side of the page were reproduced. I felt safer having the timings left in their original form, eliminating the possibility of mistakes in retyping. These copies were then given, together with the English-language timing sheets, to a typist who spoke the language fluently. She translated each line and typed it in

Italian next to its correct timing as it appeared on the sheet in English. The composer then was given copies of her sheets.

Finding a typist who could speak the language and translate was not the only problem. I couldn't find one who would also be familiar with such technical expressions as: dolly in, pan down, cut to, dissolve, and the like. Words like this are not in the normal vocabulary of a translator since they are applicable only to the motion-picture industry. I had to consult an Italian-speaking person in the industry to get exact translations for these expressions. They were then given to the typist. With a list of these expressions plus my original timing sheets, she had no trouble making up the new sheets in Italian.

Revised Timings

Always date the timings. It is not uncommon to have the picture recut after you have timed the sequences. Then, if you have to make corrections later and retime, indicate REVISED and put a new date on the sheet. You will notice this kind of information on the timing sheet of *The Bad News Bears* (page 34). This way there can be no mistakes should an old timing show up later.

If the changes are drastic, there is no choice but to completely retime, as though no timing had been done before. It may be, for example, that somewhere during the sequence the picture editor cuts out a certain amount of footage that turns out to be 0:09.3 seconds. It then remains for you to change all the following timings *from that point on* and subtract the 0:09.3 seconds from each action. But you must make sure that this changing is all he did. Even if after the footage cut you found a certain action to be 0:09.3 seconds sooner, and then found the same discrepancy at the end, you dare not assume that everything in between is the same—there may have been some shifting around. Ask the picture editor. If he tells you that he took all the 0:09.3 seconds out in one section, you know how you stand and can save yourself a lot of time and trouble. If there were a lengthening of the scene, you would then be adding the appropriate number of seconds from a certain point rather than subtracting.

Most modern electronic calculators can handle this operation very simply although they will not convert minutes. If the one you are now using has a constant function in the add and subtract mode, you can put the 0:09.3 seconds into the calculator and every time you put the old timing in, it will automatically subtract the 0:09.3 seconds and give you the new reading. If you don't have a calculator capable of performing this function you can still do what is necessary by subtracting the required amount from each old timing individually. You can also retime on the Moviola.

A word here on calculators. This is one of the most important pieces of equipment that the music editor needs. Other uses will be mentioned in this book. If you do not own one and intend to buy one, make sure it can do the above function. Request one with a constant in the addition and subtraction mode. Many calculators have this function in the division and multiplication mode only. In doing the Newman system, explained in Chapter 25 of this book, you will be using the calculator constantly.

Controlling Moviola Speed

One final word on the Moviola. It does not run at *exactly* 90 feet per minute when run with the constant-speed pedal. It runs very close to the proper speed when it is loaded down with takeups and reels and interlocked with the picture head. But when running the sound alone, without picture interlock and takeups, it runs a bit faster. This difference really has no bearing at all on practically anything for which you use the Moviola. But if you are trying to determine a true pitch you cannot get it from the sound on a Moviola. The difference between a true pitch and the pitch of a Moviola running a piece of music on the sound head alone without interlock can be as much as a half tone; the note C can be much closer to a C sharp.

On page 164 of this book is a stroboscope that will enable you to get a perfect pitch on the Moviola. You can either photocopy this from the page or draw your own. It is basically a disc of ten divisions of 36 degrees each. Like any stroboscope, it is designed to work with the frequency of the alternating-current supply, which is 60 hertz or 60 cycles per second. You can mount the stroboscope on a piece of stiff paper and tape it to the outside flange when you want to use it. To get a true pitch, put a fluorescent light very close to it so that it can be run by the variable-speed motor. Adjust the speed to where the stroboscope appears motionless. Then by using your pitch pipe at this point, the key you get will be in true pitch. Try running the sound head alone without interlock and notice how far off its speed is from the speed that gives a true pitch.

5 / What Is a Click?

35mm film runs at the speed of 90 feet per minute. There are 16 frames per foot, 24 frames per second, or 1440 frames per minute. This speed never changes. Everything in the motion picture industry is based on this set of facts.

When we speak of a 12-frame click or a 12-frame beat we refer to the elapsed interval during every 12 frames of running time, and to producing a sharp click after each interval. Since there are 24 frames per second, then a 12-frame click (12/0) is a series of clicks at ½-second intervals. A 24-frame click (24/0) is a series of clicks at 1-second intervals.

In music editing we get down to a much finer breakdown than just frames. We do not deal in just twenty-fourths of a second; we divide the second into 192 parts. Thus our work with clicks causes us to work with eighths of a frame. The difference between a 24/0 and a 24/1 is $1/192$ second, or one eighth of a frame. The difference between any tempo and the next eighth either way is also $1/192$ second.

The ear may not perceive the difference between the tempos of a 15/3 and a 15/5 click. It is two 192nds of a second, two eighths of a frame; that is, one 96th of a second. (If it were only one eighth of a frame it would be only one 192nd of a second.) This difference of one 96th of a second is practically imperceptible to the ear. It will not even change the character of the music. But it affects where your cue would finish if you had to run your music 200 beats from a given point. In these two tempos, 200 beats would end up more than two seconds apart. That is quite a difference if you must arrive at a certain point after a certain number of beats.

When working with 16mm film only the stock changes. The film runs 24 frames per second, whether it is 16mm or 35mm. The film is narrower, so the frames are smaller; consequently the footage running time of the stock changes. But the running time of any number of frames *does not change.* The 16mm film runs at the rate of 36 feet per minute as opposed to the 90 feet per minute for 35 mm. In 16mm film there are 40 frames to the foot as opposed to 16 frames to the foot in 35 mm film. You can see easily that 90 times 16 frames (90 × 16) is the same as 36 times 40 frames (36 × 40). Each is 1440 frames.

6 / The Digital Metronome and the

Indication of Click Tempos

On the scoring stage today we use a very sophisticated piece of equipment called a digital metronome. This device will produce audible clicks up to a 40/0 tempo in steps of eighths of a frame. It can be connected to as many sets of earphones as required, whether for one musician or for a whole orchestra. There are three banks of numbers that control the click tempo and these must be set by hand. The first two are for the tempo in frames and the third is for eighths of a frame. If you want to play a 12/7 click you set these controls at 127. When you push the start button the operation begins instantaneously and the time elapsed between the starting click and the second click is in the tempo for which it is set.

An important word here on referring to a tempo. When you use the expression "twelve seven" it should be written 12/7 or 12-7 but never 12.7. That last is a bad practice, for the decimal point would indicate seven tenths and most certainly that is not the meaning. If, however, you should see a 12.7 indicated, you would know that 12/7 was intended. You know that $12^7/_{10}$ makes no sense as a tempo but $12\frac{7}{8}$ does. The only really confusing tempo indication would be a 12.5. It probably *means* a 12/5 but reading 12.5 could cause one to think of $12\frac{1}{2}$, which is actually 12/4. After all, .5 is a half. It is therefore simpler to keep away from using decimal points in writing such expressions as "twelve seven" because they are mathematically incorrect. We deal in eighths of a frame, not tenths, so if you see a decimal

The Digital Metronome. It is set for 12/0.

point followed by one numeral to represent a click tempo, always question it.

There is, however, a correct way of using decimals, which is sometimes comfortable when you are figuring click tempos by the use of a calculator. When you are trying to determine the amount of time necessary for a certain number of beats, or the number of beats in a given amount of time, you will be multiplying or dividing. Using the calculator, you cannot work directly in eighths because the calculator works in the decimal system, that is, in tenths. If the calculator reads 12.7, that means 12 plus 7 tenths. So—as I explained before—the decimal point is confusing if you write 12.7 instead of 12/7 or 12-7. There is, however, a decimal equivalent of eighths and it is a true reading. You *must* indicate it in three places after the decimal point. Since it has the three places, this notation will then be accurate and can never be mistaken. Each eighth is .125 (one hundred twenty-five thousandths.) Following, then, is the proper indication for all the eighths:

$$^1/_8 = .125 \qquad ^5/_8 = .625$$
$$^2/_8 = .250 \qquad ^6/_8 = .750$$
$$^3/_8 = .375 \qquad ^7/_8 = .875$$
$$^4/_8 = .500$$

If you wish to write a 12/7 click in the decimal system, write 12.875, *not* 12.7. This way it is correct to use the decimal and there will be no confusion.

7 / Making a Set of Click Loops

Many times while timing on the Moviola, the music editor will find he needs to determine the tempo of an action such as someone walking. The composer would like to play the scene in that tempo and to catch the steps. Determining this tempo requires using click loops and every music editor should own a set. A click loop is something that you make yourself. Making a set may take a few days but you would make them only once; with care they could last for many years. A set would range from a 7/0 to a 24/0 with four clicks to each loop. They should be in eighths of a frame. You could get by with a set consisting of every other eighth—7/0, 7/2, 7/4, 7/6, 8/0, etc. A complete set in eighths would total 137 loops; the shorter set, 69. The loops can be used either for an optical system or for a magnetic system.

The optical system of sound reproduction will eventually disappear but the Moviolas have it as standard equipment. Though optical sound reproduction is greatly inferior to magnetic sound, certainly in regard to signal-to-noise ratio and frequency response, it has been industry standard for all music and sound editing since long before the introduction of magnetic sound. It is still used today as the sound reproduction system on theatrical-release prints. The sound track is printed on the release print alongside the picture. The sound is activated by a light beam passing through the track and its fluctuations are picked up by a photoelectric cell. The resulting light fluctuations are thus converted to sound energy.

An optical click track is made with a specially designed hand punch that makes three adjacent slits on opaque film stock. These slits cause a sharp click as they pass the optical beam. Exposed camera short ends or any magnetic stock that is highly opaque is good for making these tracks.

If you are starting and wish to make a set of click loops, it isn't difficult. Whether you make them optical or magnetic does not matter for the greatest part of the work. Every loop will have four clicks. The smallest loop will be a 7/0 and will be exactly 28 frames long. Each subsequent loop will be two sprockets longer. The two sprockets divided into the four clicks makes each click an eighth of a frame longer. The loops should go to at least a 24/0. You don't have to stop there if you don't want to but this should be enough. It would be difficult to make a mistake in making a loop because when the loops are one inside the other they fit perfectly and any loop that wasn't in correct position would show up instantly.

Getting the clicks is not difficult if you have access to a digital metronome and a recording studio. Start by recording the 7/0 click on a piece of 35mm stock. Push the start button on click #1 and push the stop button after click #5. Change the setting by increasing it one eighth of a frame at a time and again record five clicks. Increase the setting again by an eighth, and continue. Stop as high as you wish to go. If you have the facility to verbally slate each tempo change in-between, so much the better. When you have finished recording you will have a roll of clicks ready to be marked off, cut, and spliced into click loops. Each click will have to be marked off with the aid of a sound reader or a Moviola sound head. In putting together each loop overlap click #1 with click #5 and make your splice a bit before the click. You will then have a loop of four clicks, the fifth one being discarded. The fifth is only for the convenience of lining up with click #1 before splicing. Each loop should be checked on the synchronizer for accuracy. Each will be two sprockets longer than the previous one. By recording the clicks with the digital metronome there will be no splices in any loop except for the join.

If a digital metronome is not available, you can still make a set of loops the hard way. It would be necessary to have a full roll of equally spaced clicks to start with. You must obtain four good-sounding clicks all the same in sound quality. Make a loop exactly 6 feet long right to the sprocket. This should comprise the 4 clicks, each 24 frames apart. Then transfer this loop to a roll of 35mm stock that will be used to make your click loops. When they are transferred you will have a full

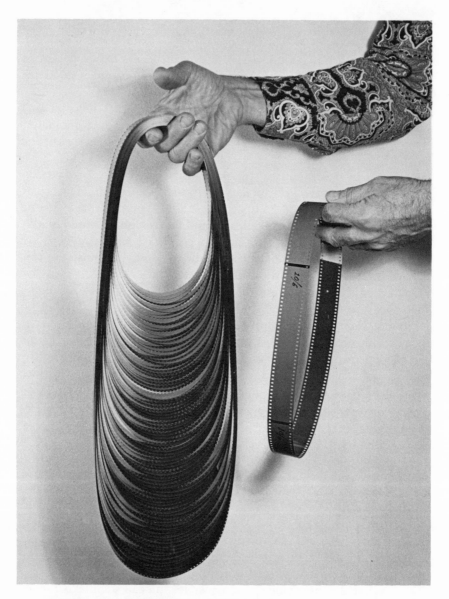

A Click Loop and a Nested Set of Click Loops

roll of clicks each 24 frames apart. Mark off the first click on the roll and run it through the synchronizer, lining up this click with any click on the loop from which it was transferred. Mark off all the clicks throughout the roll. From this marked-off roll you can now proceed to build yourself a complete set of click loops. Each loop you make is going to require careful measurements between the clicks. Since every click on the transferred roll is always going to be in the identical spot in relation to the sprocket hole, you can't make splices in odd-numbered eighths. When you are making your click loops of even eighths such as your 12/0, 12/2, 12/4, 12/6, etc., your spaces between clicks will be perfect. When making the odd-number clicks such as 12/1, 12/3, 12/5, 12/7, etc., you must alternate odd and even. In other words, in order to make a 12/1 click loop, you would alternate a 12/0, 12/2, 12/0 and 12/2. This spacing averages out to your 12/1. Similar alternation would be done throughout your set of loops on all odd click numbers. Making a set with all these splices is not the easiest way of doing it, but it beats having no set at all.

8 / Using Click Loops in Timing

When you are timing and you are fortunate enough to have a Moviola with two sound heads, it is easy to work with click loops without removing the dialogue track. If, however, the Moviola you are using has only one sound head and you wanted to use click loops, it would be necessary to put a synchronization mark on the track and picture and then remove the track temporarily in order to have the sound head free.

Let's say that we were asked to get the tempo of a walk or some other rhythmic action—someone doing calisthenics for any length of time, or someone running. Take an educated guess as to what click tempo you might need—you have to start somewhere. Take the loop you selected and line up one of the clicks with the first step and run it with the picture. It will take only a few steps before you will know if your loop is too fast or too slow. If after a few steps the click starts to precede the action, you will know the click was too fast; go back to the start and change the loop to the next slower one. This will make the synchronization a little better; you will get more of the walker's steps in tempo. Keep changing to slower and slower loops until the sync is as good as you can get. Even this will last only for short periods; nobody walks to a perfect metronomic beat for any long period. Neither does any musician or orchestra play that way. Don't ever believe that it can be done unless it was recorded to a click from a loop or a digital metronome.

This matching procedure can work either way. If the loop you start with causes the click to be late in relation to the steps, your click loop is too slow. Simply reverse the loop-selection process, trying successively faster loops.

When you have found your correct tempo, indicate on the film where it starts and what the tempo is. If the action doesn't run too long and the loop can hold it in sync, you should then be able to record with the digital metronome. If it is too long and you cannot hold it in sync throughout, the digital will not work. If the composer has decided that he wants to catch all the steps, you will then have to make a variable click track. This procedure is considerably more complicated and is explained in the next chapter.

If you have removed your sound track from the Moviola in order to use the loops, you should now go back to your sync marks and put the sound track back in sync.

9 / The Variable Click Track

Making a variable click track is more complicated than the simple use of loops. You use loops, but not in the same way. The word "variable" referring to a click track means that the clicks are not in near-perfect tempo as they are on a click loop, yet the variations in the tempo should not be noticeable unless deliberately made so as in a ritard. The adjustments or variations you make in the beats must be subtle and gradual. Any musician should be able to play to them without sounding erratic in tempo.

What makes a variable click track so called, is that the tempo changes many times throughout. You might have ten beats at a 16/5 followed by eight beats at a 16/7, and then four beats at a 16/2, and the like. As thus written, these changes look like they could be difficult to follow but they look worse on paper than they actually sound.

Synchronizing with a Varying Tempo

While timing on the Moviola we started to make a regular click track for a scene of someone walking. We found that the steps couldn't stay in sync as long as needed using a click loop, which is in perfect tempo. Since the composer wants to play in tempo to the person's walk, we must make a variable click track to match these steps. What you are trying for is to use loops that will give you the most steps before going out of sync. Here is how it works: You would choose the click loop of approximately matching tempo and run it with the picture. This part of the process is exactly as explained in the preceding chapter. Using Click Loops in Timing; review it if you need to. When you find the best matching loop, it will keep most of the steps in sync. After a certain point you will find that the click will go out of sync anyhow. It's almost impossible to go on endlessly in a perfect tempo but you will try to get as close as you can. If you're lucky you will be able to go a dozen or more steps.

Now let's say for example that you finally end up running a 12/5 click and managed to keep ten steps looking good. They start to go out of sync after this, either way. Stop here. Back up a few clicks and put a mark on the picture. The mark should be put on a click because you are going to change your loop at this point. Exactly which new loop you will use is not yet known. Starting at the click you backed up to, look at the picture while you run it from here on with this new loop, whether it is a slower or a faster one. The changed tempo will have no noticeable effect on the next few beats that worked with the other loop, but it will allow you to continue for another stretch of

A Four-Gang Synchronizer. The seconds counter is a modification not furnished by the manufacturer.

beats at this new tempo. These tempo changes are all very slight and not as drastic as you might think.

When you have gone as many beats as possible with this new loop, go back to the second mark you made when you backed up a few beats. Write the new tempo *on the picture,* using a white grease pencil. Keep up this procedure until the entire section requiring clicks has been done. You are now ready for the next step in preparation for making the track. This will be done with the sync machine. This is the common name for a synchronizer. The photo shows what would be referred to as a four-gang synchronizer. This means that four tracks or loops can be run on it synchronously. They can *not* be run independently.

Put the picture on the sync machine on the first gang. This is the one closest to you. On the third gang set up a roll of leader on which you will mark off the beats, whether they will be punched for an optical system or for cutting magnetic clicks. Be sure to put start marks on the picture and the leader. Set up your first loop on the synchronizer between these units and mark off the clicks until you reach the next sync mark. Change to the new tempo loop that you indicated on the picture. You will have to make a slight alteration where you change loops, because your picture is in frames and it was impossible to mark the exact sprocket position for the click on the picture when you had it on the Moviola. To make this alteration, when you put the second loop on the synchronizer on the correct frame you marked, do not remove the previous loop immediately. Go back to where the beats of both loops coincide. This shouldn't be any more than two or three beats. Make your change here. With luck, you may not have to go back at all; the beats might coincide where you put the loop on. If they do, so much the better. If you do have to go back and the beats separate further as you go, then go forward and make the change a few beats later where they *will* coincide. And they will, one way or the other, depending on whether you went slower or faster when you changed your tempo. When the tempos are all marked out, this roll of leader is ready for the next step in becoming the click track.

This entire operation may seem hard to comprehend as it is described in words, but a little practice in doing it will ultimately show you how it works.

After your track is all marked out, all that is left to do is to punch it with an optical click punch or to cut magnetic clicks to match the marked-out leader. Heaven help you if you have to cut magnetic clicks for any length of time. That's why I'm glad the optical system is still around.

If it turns out that the studio you are going to record in is not equipped to run optical tracks, it is a simple matter to have them transferred to a 35mm magnetic copy with start marks for the scoring stage. Then simply line up the copy to run with the picture.

Catching Action Exactly on a Beat

There is another way a variable click becomes necessary. Occasionally a composer may request one in scoring. He wants to catch scene cuts or other actions on specified beats. He knows the approximate tempo of the cue but if he works from a digital metronome click, all of the actions he would like to catch would either be before or after the beat—plus or minus several frames. He would prefer precision and he *can* have it. The variable click track is the answer. It can be calculated so that he can catch the actions on the beats he indicates, and the tempo variations will not be noticed. Doing this without a calculator would be next to impossible.

The original timing sheet that you gave to the composer might come back to you with click numbers next to the timings. To demonstrate an example of how you would compute your variable click track, it would be advisable to view the sample chart on p. 56 while reading the procedure. You can make your own similar chart. It helps simplify the operation. You must do all these calculations before doing any film work. The information you might receive could be a timing sheet with click numbers and seconds:

Click #1	0:00
Click #31	0:26
Click #72	1:02.1
Click #93	1:19.9
Click #101	1:26.7
Click #154	2:13.2 (last)

These make the first and third columns of the chart.

Each interval between the click numbers must be computed individually. This must be done in frames rather than in seconds. (A second is too big a unit, since each second comprises 24 frames.)

Computations for Making a Variable Click Track

Click Number	Intervals to Next Click	Timing	Footage	Frames to Next Click	Actual Tempo*	How to Correct	Adjusted Tempo
1	30	0:00	000	624	20.800 $20.750 \times 30 = 622.500$	Must gain 12 eighths	18 clicks @ 20/6 12 clicks @ 20/7
31	41	0:26	39+0	866	21.121951 $21.125 \times 41 = 866.125$	Must lose 1 eighth	40 clicks @ 21/1 1 click @ 21/0
72	21	1:02.1	93+2	427	20.333333 $20.375 \times 21 = 427.875$	Must lose 7 eighths	14 clicks @ 20/3 7 clicks @ 20/2
93	8	1:19.9	119+13	164	20.500	as is	8 clicks @ 20/4
101	53	1:26.7	130+1	1116	21.056603 $21.000 \times 53 = 1113$	Must gain 24 eighths	29 clicks @ 21/0 24 clicks @ 21/1
154		2:13.2	199+13				

*The number standing alone is the calculator readout, extended to at least three decimal places although the calculator does not show unnecessary zeroes. The decimal fractions in the second lines represent eighths, translated to decimal notation.

With the start of the cue on the Moviola, zero both counters. Run down to each timing with a given click number, and take down the footage and frame reading of each. Indicate this reading in the footage column (the fourth) as shown on the sample sheet. After this, everything will be computed in frames, as in the fifth column, Frames to Next Click. You must therefore determine how many frames there are between the numbered clicks. The footage from click #1 at 000 to click #31 at 39+0 is converted to 624 frames by multiplying the 39 feet by 16 frames per foot. This figure 624 is entered in the fifth column.

The next footage, for click #72, includes the 39+0 feet, so the footage between click #72 and click #31 is 93+2 minus 39+0, or 54+2. Converting, this difference becomes $(54 \times 16) + 2 = 866$ frames. You would get the same result by first getting the frame count for 93+2, which is $(93 \times 16) + 2 = 1490$ frames, and includes the 624 frames in the 39+0 footage. Subtracting, you would get $1490 - 624 = 866$ frames. The 866, whichever way you figured it, goes into the chart; the other numbers in either calculation get cleared off your calculator or dropped into your wastebasket on scratch paper when you are through with them.

Go on doing the necessary calculation through the entire column until the end. The bottom of the column has no figure since you have reached your last click and there is no next click.

The next step is to determine the tempo needed between points. We begin by finding the Actual Tempo (column 6). We know that from click #1 to click #31 there are 624 frames. We divide the 624 frames by the interval, which is 30, as listed in the second column, Intervals to Next Click. The answer is 20.800 but the closest tempo to this is at 20.750, which we refer to as 20/6. But for computing with the calculator we must use its decimal system. Knowing that 20.750 is not the exact tempo, we must measure the discrepancy and correct it. We multiply the 20.750 by 30 (intervals) and get the answer of 622.500 or 622½. This is exactly 1½ frames short or our mark (624 frames). We make up for the shortage by adding the 1½ frames in the form of eighths; 1½ is 12 eighths. (See column 7, How to Correct.) Since we need a total of 30 beats between points, we run at 20.750 (20/6) for the first 18 beats and at 20.875 (20/7) for the remaining 12 beats. (See the last column, Adjusted Tempo.) These last 12 beats were increased one eighth each and thus absorbed the balance of 1½ frames that was needed. This correction will land us exactly on the footage 39+0, where we will continue with a minutely different tempo, the difference of which will be imperceptible to most ears. The actual track will not be made until we have finished the last column.

The same kind of procedure is done between each two click points. Some adjustments may require adding and some may require subtracting in order to arrive at a given point. Once in a while you may be lucky and no adjustment will be necessary.

Before making the actual click track, you can verify all the calculations. Add up the entire last column and you will find that it totals the length of the cue in frames.

18 clicks @ 20/6	or	$18 \times 20.750 =$	373.50
12 clicks @ 20/7	or	$12 \times 20.875 =$	250.50
40 clicks @ 21/1	or	$40 \times 21.125 =$	845.00
1 click @ 21/0	or	$1 \times 21.000 =$	21.00
14 clicks @ 20/3	or	$14 \times 20.375 =$	285.25
7 clicks @ 20/2	or	$7 \times 20.250 =$	141.75
8 clicks @ 20/4	or	$8 \times 20.500 =$	164.00
29 clicks @ 21/0	or	$29 \times 21.000 =$	609.00
24 clicks @ 21/1	or	$24 \times 21.125 =$	507.00

Total frames 3197.00

The total footage of the cue is 199+13, which is 3197 frames.

Making the Click Track

You can now proceed to make the track.

If you intend to make an optical click track, you will mark the track you are going to punch with the aid of your click loops on the synchronizer. If you intend to make a magnetic click track, there are two ways of doing so. After you have determined all the different tempos in the cue, you can set a digital metronome and record directly to 35 mm stock. Then you can assemble your variable track on the synchronizer. The only splices you will have will be where the changes take place. If you record from the digital metronome, be sure to slate your tempos to eliminate any possibility of mistakes. By "slate your tempos" I mean that you will speak onto the tape the numbers that specify the tempo.

If a digital metronome is not available, you can make your clicks by transferring direct to 35mm stock from magnetic or optical click loops. The last column on the chart shows you what you must record to assemble your track.

Whatever method you use, record a bit overlength for each tempo you need.

10 / Making Click Tracks for Sweeteners

An existing orchestra or production track may have to be sweetened. The word "sweeten" is appropriately applied to the procedure of adding music or other sounds to augment an existing track—adding strings to an orchestra track, for instance, or even adding a single instrument on top of a full orchestra. If the track to be sweetened was originally done to a perfect beat there would be no problem in making your preparation setup. You would just have to find out what the click is and set the digital metronome to start with the track. If this information was not available to you, you could run click loops with the track on a Moviola with a double sound head. When you found the correct tempo it would stay in sync throughout. If the track that is to be sweetened was done wild (that is, without clicks or other time controls), then a variable click track would have to be made. The procedure is much the same as was previously explained.

You must first run the sound track on the Moviola and tap out the beats in tempo. This is done by holding the grease pencil in line next to the sound head. You keep time as you tap out the rhythm on the track. Do this through the complete track at least three times. Each time start from the top and go to the end. This will give you three sets of tapped out marks. The corresponding three in all the sets should all be relatively close to each other, certainly within a frame for all three, or even closer. You do this a few times for accuracy. You might want to do it more. The more marks you find grouped together in one spot, the more accurate your beat will be.

Since the film is in motion while you are tapping, what you imagine should be just a dot becomes a line. Every one does not have the same touch. The sharper you respond and rebound with the pencil, the shorter the line you will produce. It could be as short as two sprockets or as long as two frames. The important thing to remember is that the *start of the line* marks the beat. Don't let the length of the line misguide you. The start is what you responded to while you were tapping.

You are now about to make your click track on a synchronizer as you did in Chapter 9, The Variable Click Track. On the synchronizer, set up the orchestra track you tapped out, and some plain leader. Leave a gang inbetween for the loops; doing this will place the click loops adjacent to both the track and the leader. Again you will try to run your loops as long as possible, making notes as to where the beats start getting bad. The rest of the process in marking out your new track is identical to what you did when using the loops on the Moviola. The only thing that is different is that before, you were watching an action on a Moviola and now you are following tapped-out beats on a music track.

A sweetener click track is not always made. Sometimes the composer decides to sweeten by listening to the track itself while recording. This has been done many times. If it is in a very strict tempo he will have no trouble in following it and may even prefer this method. If the track does not have a strong rhythm, then the variable click track is an absolute necessity. Whether sweetening is done with or without a complete click track, you will need to set up a short one with a bar or two of preparatory clicks in the tempo of the existing track before the sweetening starts. This is like any orchestra leader's count off. You might be running both the track and the clicks together, or the clicks alone.

Your original track might sound as though the tempo was very even. After you have made your click track to these beats, you would probably find, if you ran the click alone, that it is not as even as you thought. If you run it with the music track, the difference won't even bother you.

11 / **The Click Track Book**

A book called *Project Tempo* has more numbers between its two covers than any book most people will ever see. It was devised by one of our pioneer music editors, Carroll Knudson. In 1966, he received a technical award from the Academy of Motion Picture Arts and Sciences for his contribution to the industry with the concept of this computer-printed book. Practically every motion-picture composer owns one, as do many other associated people in the industry.

The book deals in three factors: the click tempo, the number of beats, and the total timing involved. With the knowledge of any two of these factors you can easily determine the third.

1. If you know what click tempo you want and how long the music should run, the book can tell you how many beats you need.

2. If you know the number of beats you want and how long the music should run, the book can tell you the click tempo you need.

3. If you know the click tempo and the number of beats you want, the book can tell you how long the music will run.

Here is how you use *Project Tempo:* Each page has an entry column plus 10 vertical columns numbered from 0 to 9. The entry column, at the left side of the page, has numbers 0 to 600 from top to bottom in intervals of 10 beats. A sample sheet from the book is shown on p. 63. All timings are given to two decimal places, but only the first place is really necessary since each tenth is only about 2½ frames. The second decimal place can help you pin a cue down closer

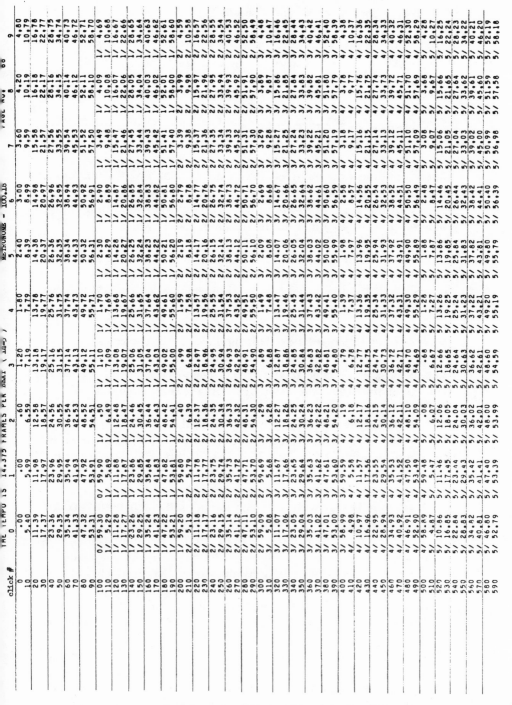

A page from the Click Track Book, *Project Tempo,* by Carroll Knudson.

to the frame. Every page of *Project Tempo* has the same organization but different information. The information starts with a 6/0 click and goes to a 36/0 click, each successive click increasing by an eighth of a frame over the preceding click. The sample page covers the 14/3 click tempo (14.375).

Let's illustrate the three examples using the sample page.

Example 1. You know that the click tempo wanted is a 14/3 or 14.375. You also know that you want to run it for 1:25.6 seconds. You want to find out how many beats you need. Look for this timing on the page of that tempo (our sample page). Following this line to the left side of the page will show 140 beats. Go back to the timing and follow it upward to the column heading and it will show 4. This means you need 140+4 = 144 beats.

Example 2. The composer told you that he wants 144 beats and he would like to run them in the time of 1:25.6 seconds. He wants to know what the tempo is. To find this information, you would have to look at beat 144 on a few pages to see what the timing is. Let us say that at random you opened to a page and when you looked at beat 144, it came at 1:30.6 seconds. This signifies that you selected too slow a page. You would then go page by page to faster tempos until you came as close as possible to the 1:25.6 seconds you are looking for. You would find that when you reached the page marked 14/3 or 14.375, that would be the correct one (again our sample). The closest tenth of the timing sheet is really all you need.

Example 3. You know that the click tempo is a 14/3 and you know the composer wants 144 beats. You want to find out how long this music will run. You then open the page marked 14.375 (14/3) and go to beat 144 and you will find that it takes 1:25.6 seconds.

A composer who wishes to play a cue and catch many actions would select the tempo and open the book to that page. He would then take his timing sheet and be able to find out on what beat each of his chosen actions would hit. They may hit exactly on beats or, if they don't, where they fit can be figured musically inbetween. The book is infallible.

Note that in the book the beats are indicated in the decimal system. Here, Mr. Knudson uses the full three decimal places, which is the correct practice.

This book is also obtainable with the time data in footage and frames instead of the seconds and hundredths shown in the sample. Both forms are available from Valle Music Reproduction, 12441 Riverside Drive, North Hollywood, California 91607.

12 / Temporary Tracks Used in Production

Many times a picture will include sequences that have some dancing scenes. Patrons in a restaurant or a night club may get up to dance, for instance. In the shooting, the director might use a commercial phonograph record to furnish a tempo that can be heard by the dancers and picked up on the set track. The records enable the people to dance, but this track is in no way intended to be final, particularly not if it is a commercial record. It is meant only to make a guide track and is to be replaced by another tune, most probably one written for the scene. The record is used not only to help the dancing look natural but also to guide everyone's dancing to the same beat. The scene would not look convincing with everyone just doing a different personal thing—unless that was the intention.

The new tune will be recorded to a variable click track, which you—the music editor—will make from this temporary track picked up on the set. The click track will be made as was explained in Chapter 9, The Variable Click Track. If, however, the track used for the dancing is an actual playback that was prerecorded, then no problem really exists. But even when there *is* an original playback for the scene and not just a guide track, the set track is a bad-quality pickup and would be replaced by the original recording. What is heard on the set track can never be good because it is played on a loudspeaker and rerecorded when shooting. Nevertheless, it must be there for the dancing.

When there is dialogue to be recorded during the dancing, the record is played and the playback is cut off just before someone has to say something. The recordist can now pick up a clean dialogue track. As soon as the dialogue is over the playback of the record is cut in again. The dancers will try to keep the steps in tempo for these intervals as though there has been no interruption. If the record had not been cut off, the dialogue would have the music under it and therefore be unusable. If the dialogue is to be looped later on for new lines, it would then make no difference if the record were to continue under the dialogue.

13 / **The Playback Recording Session**

If you have been assigned to work on a musical production, the chances are that you will be present at the recording session of the musical numbers in the show. This recording has also been called prescoring. The music editor is not always brought in at this point. It would be better if he were, but the choice is not his. If you are present, you will be doing all of the important bookkeeping. There will be logs and records kept by others, such as the mixer and the recordist, but these are for their own purposes. You will be following through with this recorded material more than they will.

One good method of identification is to use letters rather than numbers for each playback, whether it is a vocal or an instrumental. The first playback recorded would be called "A" and if take five was the selected take, it would be called "A-5". The second playback would be called "B" and followed by appropriate take numbers, and so on. These letters would always be the identification for the playbacks. If the same song in different recordings was used in the picture, the recordings would have different letters.

After the recording sessions are over and all the musical numbers have been recorded on sixteen or twenty-four track, the temporary dubdown will follow. All the selected takes must now be dubbed down for stage playbacks and other purposes. A ½-inch tape would probably be made first. It would have the orchestra divided on two channels, the vocal on another channel, and the sync pulse on the fourth channel. Nothing else may be done with the sixteen track as yet. It may be put away for future use that will include a final dubdown on 35mm three track for dubbing. This dubbing copy could very well be made from the ½-inch tape if the composer and mixer are satisfied with the balance as it is. The sixteen track will also be used to dub down later for a commercial stereo recording with a completely different balance and equalization from that used in the picture.

From this ½-inch tape a ¼-inch stage playback tape will be made with the orchestra and the vocal on separate channels. Separating the vocal and orchestra for playbacks is a very good idea. It is sometimes difficult for the performer to hear the voice when a vocal is played over the set horn because there is so much other noise on the set. The operator of the playback machine can then raise the volume of a separate vocal without blasting the orchestra at the same time.

Also from this ½-inch tape, single stripes are made on 35mm stock. These are for work purposes. The picture editor will have one; the sound on this copy is far superior to the set-track copy which he gets with the dailies. You also will be using one of these copies for synchronizing purposes before you cut your final three stripe for dubbing.

Various requests may also be coming in for cassette copies, needed for publicity or for actors wishing to rehearse at home. These would be made from the ½-inch copy.

In the event that there should be some other recorded material that will be used for playback purposes, the chances are that there may not be a sync pulse on it. If it comes from a record, then there surely is no pulse. Do *not* use this record in this form. This material should first be transferred to 35mm stock; this will be your master. Sprocket-driven material is as dependable as pulse controlled. All tape, no matter what the width, is friction driven and can be affected by temperature changes. Film can also be affected by temperature but the sprockets automatically control the running time. This control is what the sync pulse does for tape.

A picture I worked on used a commercial record for a montage. The director liked the record and was willing to pay for its use. The picture editor spent a great deal of time cutting the montage to a print made from the record. When dubbing time came around I wanted to use a fresh print. Since the record was not in good condition, I was expected to get a new copy and make a new print. The result did not match the actions in the picture as originally planned, so the picture editor had to make some cutting adjustments. Luckily he was able to. The negative had not been edited. What should have been done at the start was to transfer the record to 35mm material and then make a work copy from that. The difficulty had developed before I was assigned to the picture. It could have been prevented.

14 / Sync Pulse

The synchronizing pulse is a frequency that is recorded on tape simultaneously with other material being recorded. It is inaudible but it is a method of controlling the tape travel speed so that it runs accurately and consistently. For most recording, sync pulse is not important but in motion-picture recording it is.

Once I worked on a picture that was not a musical but did have one song in it. The song was not a playback and the sound was picked up live. It was voice and guitar only. The composer wanted to sweeten it with a small group during the regular scoring session. Though sync pulse was the last thing I should have had to be concerned with, I synchronized the original track with the picture for the scoring stage and the sweetening was a great addition. While we were recording it I thought I'd ask the engineer if we had sync pulse and he gave me a patronizing smile, as if to intimate that it was a silly question. I smiled in return, although I felt a little embarrassed to have asked. But after the session was over and the orchestra was dismissed, I got back to the question of sync pulse. The engineer was now going to put the sync pulse on an open channel of the sixteen track. *After the recording?* I knew the method would never work, but I tried it. When I got back to the Moviola with my 35mm transfer and ran it with the original track, what happened was just what I expected. The track gradually went out of sync. It ended about a foot later than the sound track it played to. We had to call the group back the next day to redo it. Luckily the scoring didn't require any precision although the sweetener did. We were also lucky that, unlike the scoring, the sweetener required only a few musicians. It could have been a lot more costly if we had to bring in a larger group.

The engineer had intended to put the pulse on the sixteen track *after* the recording and then transfer it to ½-inch tape with the pulse. I had quite a problem trying to make him understand why it had to be put on *during* the recording.

Unless you are dealing with a professional motion-picture recording studio, it is a good idea to be sure that the sync pulse is clearly understood so as to avoid any unnecessary problems.

15 / The Coding Machine

Picture editors and sound-effects editors use the coding machine, but I will discuss it only as it applies to the work of the music editor.

Coding is a time-consuming operation and shouldn't have to be your task. But unless you are on a production with a big enough editorial crew, you will not have an assistant to do the coding for you and that means you will have to take care of getting it done yourself.

The coding machine is designed to print letters and/or numbers on either edge of the film. It can be set to print one or two letters and four numbers or no letters at all. There are blanks on the letter blocks because they are stationary and do not advance as the numbers do. There are different types of coding blocks and it depends on what type was ordered with the machine. Most of them that I have seen have two letters and four numbers. When you set the machine at 0000 and thread it up it will then print consecutive numbers on every successive foot of the film—0001, 0002, and so on until the film runs out. It doesn't have to start at 0000. You individually set these numbers and you can make any number start on any frame but after that the machine pirnts them consecutively on every foot.

The start of other than 0000 will be used in coding the dailies of the playbacks before the editor gets them.

16 / Coding the Playbacks

You should have 35mm stripes of every playback in the picture besides the 35mm three track that will be used for dubbing. Each playback must be coded, and my suggestion is that the first playback that was recorded should be coded with the letter "A", the same as slated on the sixteen track at the playback recording session. Following the first "A" there should be four zeros. It really doesn't make any difference where you start to code on the track but every copy of the same playback should be coded identically, whether it is a stripe or a three track. The first modulation of music, if it is very distinct, would be the most likely place to start although the start doesn't have to be at that particular point. The reference point should be easily identifiable and if you find a good distinct sound on the track *before* the music starts, you can use this as your zero. This would then be A 0000 for the first playback.

There are many designs of coding machines. Basically they all produce the same results. Many of them have been so customized it is hard to find two that look the same, therefore no attempt will be made here to describe a machine's actual operation.

Many machines will not print with the first number on which they are set to start. They usually make their first impression on the second revolution, which would be 0001 if started from 0000. This position is perfectly all right, but if you have accidentally slipped by a few sprockets in threading up the machine, you may never know. You would see the 0001 after it printed and you wouldn't know if it were a few sprockets off. This risk can be avoided. Put a mark 2 feet before your start mark of 0000, and set your coding block to 9998. In two revolutions the numbers will have reached 0000 and the zero will print on the start frame. If you see at this time that it is not perfectly centered in the frame you can stop and start over again.

Only after you have coded the stripes does the picture editor get a copy.

Follow this procedure with all the playbacks. The second re-corded playback slated with the letter "B" would be coded B 0000 and so on.

Code the three track the same way. You will be using these codes when building the units for dubbing.

17 / **On the Set**

Your presence may be required on the set when a playback is to be photographed. The director might like to have you watch the synchronization of the performers with the playbacks. Usually, if you have been hired at the start of the playback recording, you will be present when the photography starts. You would be watching for things the director might not be aware of.

The performers in the film are not always the same performers who did the playbacks. There are countless instances where the person who recorded the track and the photographed performer are not the same.

You need also to watch for sideline musicians. They are actual musicians who are used in scenes where they are supposed to be playing, but like other performers they are just doing a playback. They may actually play at the same time but such a rendition is not recorded nor used.

There will be times when someone in the cast who is not a musician has to (supposedly) play some instrument. Often he or she does not know how to hold the instrument properly. Here also is where you can be of great help.

From an editorial standpoint, being the music editor, you should be present in case you have to come up with some answers no one else has.

18 / Coding the Dailies for the Picture Editor

After the musical numbers have been photographed there will be many reels of dailies. They will be lined up by the assistant picture editor and given a daily code. This has nothing to do with the music code you will be putting on. Just be certain that the code you will be putting on will not overlap with his. If you find that this will happen, then code on the other edge of the film.

You might have many reels of one playback only. Some or all of the takes may be incomplete. Some may start in places other than at the beginning. Some may end before the playback is over, but the entire playback will be covered in bits and pieces and in many takes. The sound track that you will receive with the dailies will be the sound picked up from the horn on the set. This is what the performers have heard. The quality is no good because all the room noise has been picked up with it. Yet this track has a good value and its uses will be explained.

You must now match this set track, which may be only a portion of the playback, to the corresponding section of the coded stripe. Look for a guitar plunk to sync to, or something else prominent, and match it right to the sprocket. This set track must now be coded identically with the stripe. You must also code the picture so that all three are in sync.

If you found that a scene was photographed starting late in the playback, where the code may be C 0165 for example, it would be necessary to code the set track the same way. This operation must be done with every take in every roll of playbacks. Since each roll of dailies has many scenes, you must keep your eye on the coding machine to be sure you stop it after each scene. The coding block will have to be reset for the next code number.

The coded dailies are then sent to the picture editor. When he cuts the picture he knows where to find any section he is looking for. He will also be cutting and keeping the code numbers in continuity and as a result he can use any portions of any take without getting into trouble. The photography will always be in sync. The picture editor can use the coded stripe. He has no complete rendition of the playback other than the coded copy you give him, unless one of the scenes was shot complete. He will follow the numbers, but his choice of scenes will be according to his personal taste in the picture editing.

19 / Final Editing of Playbacks

Normally you should have a period of free time after all the Moviola timings have been done and before you are getting ready for the scoring session. Use this time for editing your playbacks. Once you start to prepare for the scoring stage you will be very busy. You certainly should have the final dubdowns of your playbacks from the sixteen track to the three-stripe 35mm. You should also have ordered new prints of any production music tracks that may exist. Someone singing in the shower or whistling a tune would be an example. Anything of this nature would come under the heading of a music track.

Most of these production tracks are not in condition to be used for dubbing. They may be damaged or have some bad cuts in them. They may be clipped off badly at either end. You *should* order new prints for the dubbing. They should be put into the music units anyhow and not in the sound track.

The work sound track will have coded copies of the playbacks cut into it. If you should have a dupe copy of the work track, which would not be coded, then your dupe picture should show the music coding. This will transfer when the dupe is made. Before you cut in your 35mm dubdowns they should be coded to match the stripe if they have not yet been done. Cutting the dubdowns into the dubbing units is then a case of matching the numbers with the picture or sound-track coding.

Check your codes all the way through the playbacks. There may be intercutting, which will have to be done on your three tracks to match them to the stripes. If the cuts are good on the stripe copy, there is no reason to assume they will not be equally good on the three track if you match the splices exactly to the sprocket. It would still be advisable to check each three-track cut on a Moviola with a three-track head. You should have one with this type of a head on it anyhow. Some Moviolas have been so customized that not only do they have three-track heads but they also have individual switches for each channel and volume controls for each.

Another type of situation occasionally comes up on musical play-backs. I worked on one for which the original recording was on a six-teen track. It had a vocal soloist, a vocal group, and quite a large orchestra. It was dubbed down for the playback on the stage and also to the three track for the final dubbing. Later on when the picture editor finished cutting the sequence, it was fine except for some volume faults. He had made several cuts to different instrumentalists and to the vocal lead. He also cut to the group singers, who were about ten feet away from the soloist. When I looked at the finished picture with the music track, I became aware that something was missing. I would be looking at a cut to the group singers but could hardly hear them. The same situation applied when he had cut to various shots of in-strumentalists. The dubdown had good separation of the soloist on a separate channel. Everything else was combined on the other two channels, making it impossible to feature anything other than the solo-ist. Practically everyone had originally been recorded on individual tracks but our dubbing medium was only a three track. There was no other way of featuring any other performer. There also is no way of knowing during the recording how the picture is eventually going to be cut. What was done was to have the mixer go to the sixteen track and make a stripe copy of each of the closeups needed. I coded these to correspond to the three track and then cut them on separate units as they appeared on the screen. When the guitar was visual on a closeup, only this section of track used on this closeup would be cut in. The rest of the guitar stripe wasn't needed so it just went into the trim box. When there is enough space between such various featured cuts, they can be put on a single unit; otherwise, more than one unit is needed. This procedure simplifies everything for the dubbing stage.

If there is some sweetening to be done to the playbacks, use your stripe copy and build it on a separate unit as a scoring-stage guide. You could use your three track dubdown which would already be built into a dubbing unit, and send that to the stage as a guide track.

If you are in need of a 35mm transfer from another 35mm and must have sprocket-hole sync, there is a very handy aid available called tone beeps. They come in a small packet containing strips of quarter-inch tape that are adhered to peel-off backing. The strips are about four inches long. A very loud tone of about one thousand cycles is recorded on them. You can cut off a small piece about a half inch long, peel it off the backing paper, and stick it on the sound-track area of what you wish to transfer. Using this tape makes it a lot easier to line up prints than trying to find your sync on a Moviola by modulation alone. I even carry a small piece in my wallet in case I need it in a hurry. Simply put a piece about the length of a frame on the track *before* the start of what you intend to use. It will cut through loud and clear. When you get your transfer, just line up your beeps. Don't forget to remove the beep you stuck on the original.

Tone beeps should be available from any professional film-supply company in your locality. If you run into any difficulty, they can be obtained from Hollywood Film Company, P.O. Box 38536, Hollywood, California 90038. The item is called tone beeps in their catalogue, item number 5018. The cost is about $2 to $3 a packet.

20 / Hand Claps; Nonmusical Sweetners

There may be sequences in which various people can be seen clapping hands or snapping fingers in time to the music. If this sequence was shot with the actual playback that is to be used, there is no problem. The claps and snaps picked up on the set track would most probably be all you would need. It's true that the playback would also be heard on the set track, but when you cut your final track on top of this it will most likely overshadow the music on the set track, though a lot depends on how loudly the music was played during the shooting. The combination of these two tracks gives a realism that seems to be missing without some of the set track underneath. I have heard musical numbers in pictures and it was very obvious to me when the playbacks would start. The character of the sound changed suddenly. The naturalness disappeared. To avoid this, I always cut the set track in but it is not always used. When it is, it is kept very low, and it should be.

If the music on the set tack was used strictly for tempo and the tune was not meant to be used at all, then you couldn't use these claps. You would have to arrange to assemble a suitable number of people to do the clapping and finger snapping and then record them to the set track. This recording would give you a clean clapping track without music. It should be done on an ADR stage if one is available. The tune to be finally used would then be done to a click track made from the set track. Doing this puts everything in sync.

At this point I should explain what the ADR stage is. The ADR (automatic dialogue replacement) stage is a recording studio set up with special equipment for replacing the dialogue of performers in the film. There could be numerous reasons for doing this: The dialogue may have been originally recorded with bad quality. The director might want to redo lines because he wanted to get a better reading or to eliminate unwanted noises in the original. The ADR stage would also be used for recording the dialogue in various languages for release in foreign countries.

The ADR stage also has projection, which is necessary for this procedure. The performers wear headphones to hear what they are replacing. They rehearse to the old track they will replace and then record the new one.

Years ago the replacing of dialogue was done by a method called looping. The expression is still used today, but not the method. This involved making synced loops of the picture and track of each line you wanted to redo. They would be recorded individually and then cut into the sound track for final dubbing. After this procedure you then had to open the loops and reassemble the picture and track unless you had a dupe made just for this purpose. Today with ADR, neither picture nor track is cut up in any way. Computer technology has taken over. The starts and stops of each line of dialogue are determined by an editor who specializes in this type of work. The film will start, stop, and reverse at the proper footages based on the information supplied by the editor. The rest is automatic. The performer's new line is ready for recording; then on to the next line without touching the film.

No one can disagree with the fact that the modern-day method is very much faster, not even those who will not use it. And there are many motion-picture stars who will not use this method of voice replacement. They feel that the method by which the ADR system operates is completely soul-destroying because of its mechanization. They prefer the original conventional method of looping, which they feel allows them to redo their original lines with more feeling.

Since this kind of a studio is ideal for doing hand claps, it should be used whenever possible. So much for the ADR stage.

Hand clapping is something that should be controlled by the music editor and not by the sound-effects editor. The claps must be rhythmic, and if a sound-effects editor does the editing he is guided by what he sees, which may not be the best choice even though it may be more correct. The claps could be cut visually and could be run with the picture and *look* perfect. But if you then ran the music track and the claps together there is a very good change that what you heard would disturb you greatly. There must be a musical marriage between the claps and the music, even if the claps are not on the exact frame pictorially. You will not be as aware of this discrepancy as you would be if the claps and the music were not in tempo *to each other.*

A slight shift of the picture may be in order occasionally. Suppose you have a cut to people clapping. You have already recorded claps to the music, but on this cut, the claps you see are four frames later than those you hear. The picture editor can help you here. He could probably trim the first four frames from the head of the scene and add them at the end, thereby keeping his overall footage of the scene the same as before. He could also do the shifting in reverse if the situation warranted it. This way of solving the problem of synchronizing the claps has been done numerous times.

Some additional information on hand clapping or anything similar:

If you need many clappers and have only a few people to record with, you cannot make a small number of claps sound like a lot by using many prints of them and building them on many tracks. Staggering them a few sprockets, or similar tricks, does not work. It has been tried many times and is not successful. There is a way to do it and I would like to explain the logic behind it.

You could not take twenty prints of one violin solo performance from the same master, put them on twenty reproducers, and have the combination sound like twenty violins, because it will not. It never can, because the prints are all the same. No trick you can employ will change this. Why then do twenty violinists in a symphony orchestra sound like twenty? Because they all have different tones; there would never be two identical renditions. But there *is* a way to make a single violinist sound like twenty. He *can* become twenty different violinists by having him record the same solo twenty times. Sync these prints up on twenty reproducers. This will do what you need.

The same applies to hand claps. After you have your group do the claps, make another recording and then another. Use them all if you wish. Each time they clap they are not the same people.

To elaborate even further, there is a way to make the same print sound like more *without* recording it more than once. This can only be done with something like claps and not with music; you will readily see why.

Make two prints of the claps from the same master. Line them up so that the first one starts where it should. Take the second print and have the first clap on this print line up with the second clap of the first print. This way you have twice as many people clapping. The clappers become different people all the way through. They are never clapping on print #2 with the same clap on print #1. There is therefore no duplication of sound anywhere. The only thing you have to watch out for is tempo changes. Staggering these tracks as you are now doing could require a frame or two of adjustment on the second print every once in a while.

There is actually nothing difficult about cutting a series of claps or finger snaps taken from a library, but if a great deal of cutting is necessary it could take forever. You would have to first tap out your music track as you did before; you must have something visual to cut the claps to, so your tapped-out beats would be what you would follow in making the cuts. It is much simpler to record to picture and thereby get a splice-free and more natural sounding track. This way, of course, is always preferable, but many conditions could prevent you from recording the claps live. If you do cut them, it is a good idea after you have finished to transfer this cut copy to another copy without splices. One accident with all those splices in the high-speed rewinding of the machine rooms, and you've had it!

When you set up your dubbing units and cut these claps or other sounds in, you will probably get a single stripe from the transfer department unless you request full coat. Such single stripes should not be cut into any units containing three-track stock. The reason for this is for compliance with sound department requests. Since a three-track head spans the entire width of 35mm film, a single head spans only the left channel. As a result, the stripe that is run on a three-track machine causes uneven wear of the three-track head by the stripe passing over one head only. If you have any reason for wanting to cut this track into a unit containing three track, have your transfer put on full coat on the left channel only.

The article on page 85 recently appeared in the *Los Angeles Times*. It is a partial explanation by Miss Eleanor Powell of how tap dancing is done for motion pictures.

Miss Powell's description of the procedure is basically correct and it would not have been expected of her to elaborate further. The article made good reading for the newspaper and was really all that was necessary for the public. The last paragraph skims very lightly over the most important aspect of this work. As a music editor I found it difficult to accept the phrase: "She would go back to the recording

---

Complicated Process

Powell, one of the great tap dancers of the great tap-dancing films, described the process movie dancers went through. She, like Fred Astaire, choreographed her own numbers. After working out the steps, she did the number in ballet slippers for the orchestra in the recording studio "to help lead the number tempo-wise."

Then would come the filming of the dance: "This is always done silently, primarily because of the cost. The cameras have to move all over the set when you're dancing and there's quite a lot of noise. Someone might sneeze, someone might cough, and the language they use . . ."

It was only after the picture was shot and edited that she would go back to the recording studio and synchronize her taps. "That's the hard part. You have to remember the routines with all those intricate little tap steps."

—Copyright, 1979, *Los Angeles Times,* Sept.
12, 1979. Reprinted by permission.

studio and synchronize her taps." This is an indication that the taps already exist when in fact they have not even been recorded at this point.

The procedure is as follows: The dancer would go back to the recording studio and *record* the tap steps. A music editor would also be present. The dancer would do the steps on a wooden floor and a microphone placed near the floor would pick up and record the steps. The dancer listens to the recorded orchestra on earphones while watching the picture and doing the steps. Earphones must be worn by the dancer so that a clean recording of the dance steps alone can be made. The orchestra will not be recorded on the track with the steps. They will not be combined until the dubbing. This separation permits the dubbing mixer to control the balance between the steps and the orchestra.

Even the best of dancers may sometimes find it difficult to remember all the steps he or she did even while watching the picture. The dance routine would probably be recorded many times and not one single rendition would be good in its entirety. The final and acceptable sound track of the tap steps usually ends up with many splices, combinations of many takes. As an example, it might start out with 8 bars from Take 2, followed by 16 bars from Take 3, followed by 4 bars from Take 1, and so on. This would not be unusual. Intercutting tap steps is really not any different from the intercutting of, vocal or music tracks.

After the recording of the steps, some artists prefer to work closely with the music editor at the Moviola. They might like to try the different takes with the music track and select which portions of which takes to use.

It is only fair to mention that this does not take anything away from the skill of the artist. The difficult task of trying to recreate what was photographed and doing the steps at a later time necessitates this intercutting.

21 / **Bar Charts**

In addition to timing sheets, or instead of them, bar charts are a form in which a composer may receive his information to write cues. Usually a timing sheet accompanies the bar chart, but not always. As explained in the use of the click track book, the beat number of an action can be determined in any tempo. Some composers will make their own bar charts but some may expect you to do it. The composer may say that he wants a certain cue laid out on a bar chart and he would give you the tempo. The tempo is the one thing he *must* give you. Then with the timing sheet and the click track book, you would open to the page of the tempo he selected and put the actions down on the proper beats or show their closest relationship to the beat. There are many ways you can make bar charts but the manner of putting the information down would essentially be the same no matter which type you use.

On page 88 is a sample first page of timed cues from *The Bad News Bears*. We will use this to demonstrate how to put it on a bar chart. The composer may request that you use a chart with no bar lines because he really doesn't know how he wants to write the cue at this point. He may wish to write the cue in 3/4 or 4/4 time or whatever else may suit his fancy. The following cues from the timing sheet have been laid out on the bar chart (page 89) with no bar lines. This allows using a mixture of bars in 5/4, 4/4, and 3/4 time in any sequence. We

CUE __M 93___   SCORING START ___123+0___

TITLE ___The Astrodome_____   CLICK TEMPO _14/3_____

STARTS AT __142+5__ IN REEL   WARNING CLICKS __8____

DATE __June 20th 1977__

0:00	SEGUE from 1:03.3 Cue M92 as kids get up to greet Kelly.
0:05.1 0:06.8	Kelly shouts: "What does this mean for the Toros?"
0:07.3	Cut to Mike as kids cheer.
0:09.4	Cut to M.S. Mike getting up as they start to leave locker room.
0:11.3	Cut to the kids charging out of the locker room.
0:14.7	Cut to kids running out on the field. Camera pulls back.
0:24.7	End pull back revealing the whole Astrodome.
0:32.1 0:34.8	Cut to Orlansky in seat with his girl friends. He says: "That's the kids I told ya about from California."
0:35.3	Cut to Toby looking straight up and turning slowly. He is astounded by the place.
0:38.7	Cue to his point of view of the dome. Turning.
0:41.7	Cut to a downward shot of him looking up and turning.
0:43.8	Dizzy, he falls and hits ground.
0:44.9	Cut to Ahmad.
0:46.8	He turns to look at sign not yet in focus.
0:47.3	It focuses. CF No.44. AHMAD ABDUL RAHIM.
0:49.2	Cut to C.U. Ahmad. He can't believe it.

A Timing Sheet for *The Bad News Bears*. This corresponds to the bar chart for the same cues.

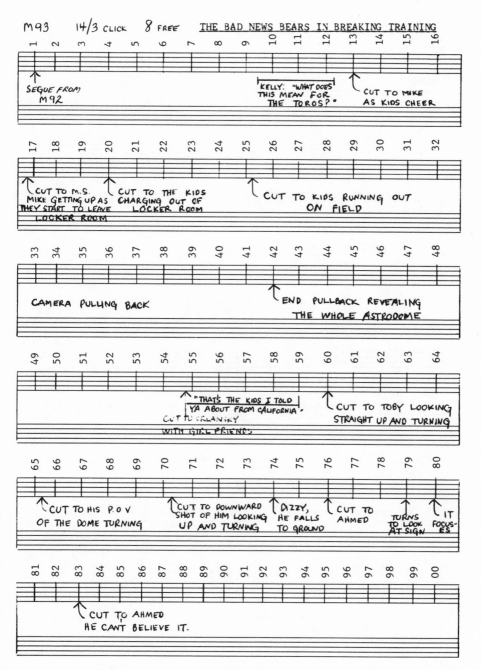

A Bar Chart: *The Bad News Bears*. This corresponds to the timing sheet for the same cues.

PRODUCTION TITLE

CLICK TEMPO

SEQUENCE

TOTAL TIME

| 1 | 2 | 3 | 4 | 5 | 6 | 7 | 8 | 9 | 10 | 11 | 12 | 13 | 14 | 15 | 16 |

1   2   3   4

| 17 | 18 | 19 | 20 | 21 | 22 | 23 | 24 | 25 | 26 | 27 | 28 | 29 | 30 | 31 | 32 |

5   6   7   8

| 33 | 34 | 35 | 36 | 37 | 38 | 39 | 40 | 41 | 42 | 43 | 44 | 45 | 46 | 47 | 48 |

9   10   11   12

| 49 | 50 | 51 | 52 | 53 | 54 | 55 | 56 | 57 | 58 | 59 | 60 | 61 | 62 | 63 | 64 |

13   14   15   16

| 65 | 66 | 67 | 68 | 69 | 70 | 71 | 72 | 73 | 74 | 75 | 76 | 77 | 78 | 79 | 80 |

17   18   19   20

Alpheus Music Corp
Hollywood. Calif.   SP-402

DATE _____

A Bar Chart. Alternative form, marked 4/4 time.

will assume that the tempo the composer selected is a 14.375 (14/3). This tempo is used for this demonstration simply because this is the sample page we have of the click track book shown and described earlier. If you will compare the sample timing sheet for *The Bad News Bears* and the sample 14/3 page of the click track book (page 63 of this book), you will see how to write up a bar chart.

Beat 1 is the start and naturally the 0:00. The next information on the sheet is a line of dialogue starting at 0:05.1 and ending at 0:06.8. Looking on the click track page you will find that 0:05.1 comes about midway between beat 9 and beat 10. The end of the dialogue, 0:06.8, ends a bit past beat 12. The scene cut at 0:07.3 is within a tenth of a second of beat 13. Being this close, it is indicated as being *on the beat.* That's the way the entire cue is laid out. You can be fancy if you like and use blue or red for the dialogue indications.

The bar chart on page 89 shows another form. The beat numbers are indicated as in the previous sample but this chart has bar lines and can be used only for 4/4 time. Not only are the beat numbers indicated but the bars are numbered also. The chart is also double staved, allowing the composer the flexibility of using one staff for some quick sketching. The sample is left blank but the information would be put down in the same manner shown in the chart without bar lines. This sample page is only the first in a series that runs for 300 bars. Each page naturally is different. The sample page with no bar lines is a single sheet because the zeros after 99 become the next hundred and all you have to do is add the hundreds digit at the start of each succeeding page. You would not use this second type of chart without first checking with the composer. If he tells you that the cue will be written in 4/4, then you can use it. Occasionally you may have to make up your own chart if the composer wants a bar chart in 3/4, but most of the time these two types will solve any of your needs.

A bar chart can also be made directly from the Moviola; the information does not have to come from a timing sheet. You can sit at the Moviola with the click track book and, as you take off your reading of the actions, go directly to the book and then to the bar chart.

There is still another way of making a bar chart but this is necessary only if you do not have a click track book in your possession. Take the loop of the selected tempo and mark off all the beats on a piece of leader. Number them consecutively as you mark them off. You can then put this marked-off leader on the sound head of the Moviola and take your reading of beat numbers from this as you view the picture. You would need the Moviola with a double sound head. If you have only a single sound head, you can write your beat numbers on the sound track before starting instead of using the leader.

22 / **Preparation for the Scoring Session**

After all your timings and bar charts are done for the composer, besides anything else he may have you do, you will be starting to get ready for the scoring session. Some composers will either sit down with you and go over everything or else give you all the information on the telephone that you need in order to set up everything for the scoring session. Sometimes a composer is too busy, even up to the last moment, so it becomes up to you to get anything prepared without even talking to him.

He will be sending in his scores to the copyists in the music department. You will then have to determine what is needed by reading the scores yourself. A very experienced composer will have everything on the score. The score will say at the top what the click tempo is and how many warning clicks there will be, such as 8 warning if the music is in 4/4 or 6 warning if the music is in 3/4. You had better check through every page. He may decide not to carry the clicks all the way through, but may want you to shut them off at the last quarter of bar 35, for instance. If you are a musician you will have no trouble following the score. If you are not a musician you will have to count clicks, but you will also have to see that there are no 5/4 or 3/4 bars in the cue or your count will be off.

There might be a cue in which the composer started out in free time and then decided to bring in the click later in the cue. He would write his music so as to accommodate the click entrance. He would not likely have any warning clicks over music in a different tempo than the click. The warning clicks would usually be heard during a fermata preceding the clicked section. There have been occasions where the composer didn't want *any* warning clicks prior to going into the clicked section; they would have interfered with the preceding tempo and he had no intention of having a fermata just for convenience. He wanted to start the digital metronome on cue just as he went into the clicked section. Since they would have an idea of what the incoming tempo was going to be, this lack of warning did not faze the musicians or the composer. They knew what to expect and caught the tempo instantly.

I have found cues where there were multiple starts and stops of the clicks, each one at a different tempo. The cue started with a click and had to be stopped at a designated point in order to go into free timing. While the free timing was being played I had to change the setting on the digital metronome for the next tempo. This practice is not common but a cue like this can keep you pretty much on your toes. I have cited this merely as an example of an uncommon procedure that could arise.

Some studios are equipped to start the digital metronome mechanically. There is a method where the metronome can be started by the projection machine. You place a piece of silver reflective foil on a designated frame of the picture. As the film advances, the foil passes a triggering device in the projector and activates a switch by the reflection of a light beam on the foil. This starts the metronome. You must stop it manually.

There is another and better method. It's better because you don't have to bother putting foil on the picture. It has the further advantage that if you need to do so you can make a last-minute change. You won't have to run to the projection room to remove the old foil and put on a new piece. This system is made by Veeder-Root, the company that makes the footage and seconds counters for Moviolas and synchronizers. It is a digital control and is called an Econo-Flex. You calculate the number of frames from the start mark to where you want the first click to start. You give this frame count to the person who operates the digital control. He programs this number into his machine and it starts counting when the projector and recording machine start. It starts the metronome at the precise number of frames you set it for. Stopping the clicks is manual as before, but the precision is needed for starting, not stopping.

When using clicks, it is a good idea to put a streamer at the start of the warning clicks. A streamer is a scribed line on the picture that starts on the left side of the screen and travels across to the right side through three feet of film. When this line reaches the end, it is the cue for the start of the music or warning clicks, or anything else it may be intended for.

At the end of each streamer you punch a hole in the frame. This adds to the visual impact of the end of the line. For the warning streamer, go over the scribe with a colored marker (I favor blue). This way the composer knows that when the streamer starts, it is for the start of the warning clicks and that he hasn't missed the down beat. He will also use it to start the count-off for the orchestra.

In establishing where the first warning click is to start, you first select your loop of the tempo you need. On the synchronizer, place the frame on which the music is to start in sync with any beat on the loop. Back up to the required number of warning clicks you need. This frame will be where they start.

The warning streamer is not necessary when the clicks are started by the Veeder-Root counter, but put it on anyhow. Can you imagine what would happen if the Veeder-Root starter did not work for any reason? Protect yourself. You can always start the digital metronome yourself if you have placed a visual streamer.

A composer may give you the scoring preparation on the phone. He might say: "Give me a streamer at the start, one at 0:06.3, one at 0:34.5 and one at the end." As he gives them to you, circle them in red on your copy of the timing sheet.

Some composers never use clicks and will catch all the actions with streamers. Their scores will have timings on some of the bars and by following the clock they can maintain their correct tempo and then look up to the screen for the streamers. Cues have been prepared that had as many as a dozen lines scribed within a 1-minute cue. As another extreme, there have been cues that simply had a streamer at the start and one at the end; the composer does the rest with the clock.

As you are preparing each cue you will need to put a start mark for the scoring stage on both the work track and the picture. Put them about 15 feet before the start streamer of a cue if there are no clicks. If there are warning clicks, put the streamer 15 feet before the start of the warning clicks. This gives ample time for the machine to get up to speed and gives the stage man time to slate the cue.

You will have put start-mark tapes on both the picture and the dialogue track, and it is a good idea to write on these not only the cue number but also the footage on which it starts.

The First Page of a Composer's Music Sketch. Note the streamers indicated to end at 0:00, at 0:23.3, at 0:42.1, at 1:14, and at 1:25.

ORCHESTRA CHART

PRODUCTION: HEAVEN CAN WAIT No. ____ 5/11/76 9:30 A.M. STUDIO "M"

SCORER: DAVE GRUSIN   CONDUCTOR: DAVE GRUSIN

SEQUENCE	COMPOSITION	TIMING	COMPOSER	ARRANGER	VIOLIN	VIOLA	CELLO	BASS	FLUTE	OBOE	CLARINET	SAX	BASSOON	HORNS	TRUMPETS	TROMBONES	TUBA	HARP	PIANO	DRUMS	GUITAR	SAX W/INC. SAX	TOTAL
1037/201A	HEAVEN WALK	1:56	DAVE GRUSIN	DAVE GRUSIN	12	6	4	2	2	1	2		1	3	1		1	1	2	2	1	1	42
205	WALK TO HOUSE	:29	"	"	12	6	4	2	2	1	2		1	3	1		1	1	2	2	1	1	42
501	MEETING OF THE BORED	:46	"	"	12	6	4	2	2	1	2		1	3	1		1	1	2	2	1	1	42
502	TO THE MEETING	:15	"	"	12	6	4	2	2	1	2		1	3	1		1	1	2	2		1	40
906	LAST WALK	:52	"	"	12	6	4	2	2	1	2		1	3	1		1	1	2	2	1	1	42
901	GARDEN WALK	1:44	"	RICHARD HAZARD	12	6	4	2	2	1	2		1	3	1		1	1	2	2	1	1	42
1202	END TITLES	2:25	"	DAVE GRUSIN	12	6	4	2	2	1	2		1	3	1		1	1	2	2	1	1	42
401A	DINNER AT EIGHT	:47	"	RICHARD HAZARD	12	6	4	2	2	1	2		1	3	1			1	1	1			35
801	TRAINING MONTAGE	1:41	"	"	12	6	4	2	2	1	2		1	3	1			1	1	1		1	38
904	GOODBYE	1:38	"	"	12	6	4	2	2	1	2		1	3				1	1	1			37
1005	STADIUM TRANSITION	:41	"	DAVE GRUSIN	12	6	4	2	2	1	2		1	3	1				2	2	1		38
1102	GOODBYE MR. JORDAN	:40	"	"	12	6	4	2	2	1	2		1	1 1	1			1	1		1		34
902	MARRY ME	:29	"	RICHARD HAZARD	12	6	4	2	2	1	2		1	1 1				1	1		1		32
903	BAD NEWS	:30	"	"		6	4	2	2	1	2			3					1		1		22

An Orchestra Chart. Note that the left column does not have the cue numbers in consecutive numerical sequence.

HUBIE ⚬ — X.47

Remember that when it is completely dependent on you to get all the information from the score, you should take your time and check everything. The composer will not have the opportunity to see the streamers or hear the clicks until he steps onto that podium and starts to direct an orchestra costing many thousands of dollars per hour. You just cannot afford any mistakes in preparation. It wouldn't hurt to run the film on the Moviola after you have prepared everything so that you can actually see what you have done.

Keep a book with all your timings. When you prepare a cue, all information should be on the timing sheet—the start mark, footage, click tempo, number of warning clicks, and anything else you deem pertinent. This book is your bible.

On page 96 is a sample of a music sketch that shows how the composer usually indicates his streamers—he has drawn them in heavy black lines to points listed in the illustration caption.

Following the sample sketch is a typical orchestra chart prepared by the music department. This is the order in which you will record the cues. The log *you* sent to all personnel gives the *numerical sequence* of all the cues in the picture, but the *recording sequence* comes from the orchestra chart. It is prepared for economic reasons. Without proper planning of the sequence for recording cues, a session could run into overtime needlessly for some of the musicians. It is also possible that the copyists may still be copying some of the cues while the session is going on, a procedure that would put the recording of these cues near the end of the list.

Making a Line Scriber or Streamer Board

The streamers are usually 3 feet long (2 seconds). Some composers like slower lines, for which a 4-foot streamer would be used. The streamers are scribed through the emulsion with a sharp instrument as the film is held in place on a specially designed board. These boards are usually made to order. I don't believe they have ever been made for sale commercially. For the benefit of anyone wishing to make his own, I will try to give all the important information necessary. With this information and the drawing of the line scriber, also referred to as the streamer board, a fairly handy person should be able to build one.

To start with, you will need two pieces of clear hardwood such as

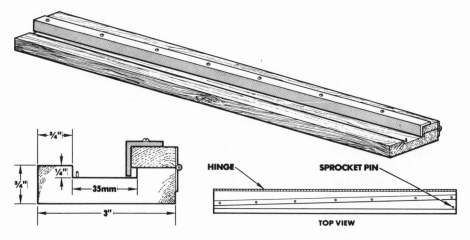

A Line Scriber or Streamer Board

ash, birch, or oak. Each piece should be 3 feet long by 3 inches wide. One should be ¾ inch thick and the other should be ½ inch thick. You will also need either a piece of angle aluminum ⅛ inch thick with an inside measurement of ¾ inch or a flat piece of aluminum stock ⅛ inch by ¾ inch. Either is to be 3 feet long.

Notice on the drawing that the aluminum does not run parallel with the edge of the board. The exact placing of this aluminum when mounted on the upper section is something you must determine while you are constructing. All you need to know is the purpose of it.

The groove in the ¾-inch piece of wood must be done with great care, using a dado or a router. This is the first step and if you overcut in width, you might as well start over with another piece of wood. The depth should be ¼ inch and the exact width should be the width of 35mm film. When the film is placed in the groove, the fit should be just right so that there is no side play. Neither should the groove be so narrow as to buckle the film.

If you choose to use the flat piece of aluminum stock, it should be screwed to the ½-inch piece of wood with flat-head screws. Countersink the screws, as this will be the edge along which you will be pulling the scribing tool. Screws should be about 6 inches apart. With the flat strip of aluminum you must be extremely careful because any adjustments after completion would be almost impossible.

Angle aluminum is not necessary, but it could make final adjustments easier. It would be fastened with screws on the top instead of the side. Make slightly oversized holes and use round-head screws. Thus they will permit the aluminum to be moved slightly if need be, after the scriber has been completed.

The other edge of the ½-inch wood must be accurately cut so that both pieces can be hinged with a section of piano hinge.

After you have mounted the aluminum, lay a piece of film in the groove, with the emulsion side up. Lay the top section with the aluminum over it. The correct angle will have to be adjusted by trial and error.

You will need a scribing tool. This can be a pin punch ground flat on a grindstone. Use one that is either ⅛ inch or ³/₁₆ inch in diameter at the ground end.

With the film in place, make some sample scribes in the emulsion by holding the scribing tool at an angle and drawing the ground side along the film and against the aluminum. Since the two sections have not yet been hinged together, you will need a C clamp at each end to hold both pieces in place until the final position can be determined. The exact setting should be such that the scribed line of removed emulsion will start the streamer on the left side of the screen and end it on the right side. The scribed line will not cut into the sound-track area, which does not show on the screen; it is masked off. The line will run at an angle across the picture areas of 3 feet of film. This will make the streamer appear on the screen as moving from complete left to complete right.

After you have experimented with many scribes and have the exact position for the top section, you are ready to prepare for hinging the sections together.

Very carefully measure how to cut off the excess wood on the edge of the top section so that it lines up with the bottom section to which it will be hinged. Take your time; this measurement is the most important one. If it is not done correctly, your line will not start and stop as planned. After cutting off the excess you can hinge the two sections together.

The last thing to be done is to make a sprocket pin to insert in the bottom section. This will hold the film from slipping while the scribing is being done. It can be made from a 16-penny nail filed to the section conformation of a sprocket tooth. It is then force fitted into an accurately positioned hole in the bottom section where you will start to scribe. Put this pin on the side away from the hinge as shown so that it doesn't interfere with the closing of the scriber. It should be put in so that when the stock is in place, the pin will go through a sprocket hole.

Any other refinements or improvements you wish to make are matters of personal preference. You have been given only the basic information needed for constructing the line scriber.

23 / Stage Logs and Guide Tracks

When you are going on the scoring stage you should prepare logs for the use of all personnel involved: the recordist, the machine-room loader, the projectionist, the mixer, the music contractor, the conductor, and yourself, plus a couple of extra copies. Someone is always needing one. These logs should give all the information necessary. Looking at the illustrated example (page 103) you will see that the projectionist can find his starts in the Start column. The music contractor needs the titles of each cue for his report (Title column). The recordist knows how long the cues run so that he doesn't run (Timing column) out of recording stock in the middle of a take. In this session all clicks were manually started. If it had used the Veeder-Root starts, there would have been a special column just for the person handling that work; it would indicate the number of frames necessary to activate the clicks.

On cue M61 and M62, the machine-room operator knows that he has a special unit to thread up for variable clicks and that they are not coming from the digital metronome. With all this information, you should be answering a lot fewer unnecessary questions.

As far as guide tracks are concerned, they would be set up the same way for the scoring stage as sweeteners would. They might not even be running during the recording but just listened to for reference. One film that I worked on had a string quartette playing at a recital. It had to be replaced because it was photographed to a com-

TITLE	CUE #	START	CLICK TEMPO	WARNING CLICKS	TIMING	RECORD WITH	PLAYBACK WITH
Main Title	M11	11+0	8/0	8	1:41	Picture-Digital	Picture-Track
Mr. Manning	M12	240+15	11/1	4	0:25	" "	"
Kelly's Bike Part I	M13	530+4	8/0	8	0:32	"	"
Kelly's Bike Part II	M13A	577+14	8/0	8	1:10	"	"
Lupus Part I	M14A	679+5	25/6	5	0:51	"	"
Lupus Part II	M14B	759+4	19/3	4	0:28	"	"
They're Off	M21	553+5	8/3	8	0:53	"	"
Kelly's Reverie	M31	503+0	None	None	0:55	Picture only	"
Smoke Signals	M41	162+11	10/6	8	0:38	Picture-Digital	"
Indian Victory	M42	548+10	14/0	4	1:18	"	"
A Cruddy Pitcher	M43	668+6	None	None	0:36	Picture only	"
The Dome	M51	9+0	None	None	1:08	" "	"
Vacancy	M52	294+0	18/0	4	0:55	Picture-Digital	"
Kelly's Dad	M53	588+0	None	None	0:56	Picture only	"
The Practice Part I	M61	289+0	Special 13/7	4	1:02	Pic.-Optical Clix	"
The Practice Part II	M62	352+0	Special 12/4	4	0:20	" " "	"
The Champs	M63	511+4	None	None	0:58	Picture only	"
The Hilton	M71	207+8	16/3	6	0:15	" "	"

The First Sheet of a Log for the Music Recording Session or Scoring Session mercial record and there was no license to use it. The use of the music was free because it was in the public domain but the actual recording could not be used. It was visual throughout and had to be in perfect sync. A variable click track had to be made for the recording. This was made from the set track, which is also the guide track sent to the scoring stage. It was run with the picture so that the musicians could get the feel of what they were going to replace. They had to do more than just read the music. There were a few necessary sour notes that had to be played at a certain point because there were some visual reactions to them. These sour notes did not appear in the record used for the playback but they were always planned to be put in later.

24 / Special Setups for Cues between Reels

When scoring a cue that plays between reels, it should be combined to score in one piece. It will have to be split up later for the dubbing but that will be after you have recorded it and checked it against the special unit you are going to build.

A cue 6M4/7M1 would naturally be the last cue in reel 6 and would continue in the beginning of reel 7. Borrow from the head of reel 7 the 7M1 portion of the picture and track that you need. Attach this section to the end of reel 6 so that the cue can be scored in one piece. Replace with blank leader what you borrowed from the head of reel 7, of the same length in order to keep reel 7 in sync.

If the 7M1 portion you borrowed turns out to be too long and reel 6 then becomes too big to handle, you should make a special unit. Completely remove the 6M4 portion and the 7M1 portion from each of the reels. Put them together, forming a special recording unit called 6M4/7M1. Do this to both the picture and track. Fill out the balance of reel 6 also with blank leader just as you did the head of reel 7.

After the scoring session you can take the special units apart and put the reels back together again with the borrowed sections. It isn't necessary that you do put them back together if you don't want to. Since you filled out the reels you can build your dubbing units the way the reels are. Your copy of the picture and sound track most probably will not be used for dubbing. The sound-effects editor's copy is usually used because he has many cues indicated on the picture for the dubbing mixer, including some streamers and punches. If no dupes were made, then most certainly you will have to reassemble the picture before dubbing.

This special setup should be put together, whether the cue goes between an A to B reel or a B to A reel.

25 / **The Newman System**

An excellent system of scoring preparation, which originated at Twentieth Century-Fox, is referred to as the Newman system. Alfred Newman was certainly a champion in the field of motion-picture scoring and this is the way he preferred to have the film prepared. It uses no clicks at all. The timing is completely free and gives the conductor the freedom he wants. He doesn't even need the clock if he doesn't want to use it; the screen is his clock and keeps him in control of his tempo. A Newman setup is complicated to prepare and very time consuming. A great deal of mathematics is used in this type of preparation and not too many composers use this system. Although I've known about it for years I never learned to use it until I worked with Al Newman on *The Greatest Story Ever Told* many years ago.

Here is how the preparation is done. The composer finishes his sketch and sends it to the music department. The music editor gets a copy. It will be noticed that the composer has indicated anchor points on the score where he wants streamers. He has also put the timings down on these points. He might also put down the approximate beat such as 26/0, but he does not mean he wants any clicks. These marks are just for reference.

A sample sketch of a scoring cue is illustrated. As the system is explained it would be helpful to keep referring to the sketch.

Looking at the music, you will notice that there is a streamer at 0:00. There are also anchor points with streamers at 0:48, 1:13.1,

1:43.3 and the end at 2:04.6. This is all the composer sends in as far as information is concerned. He means to conduct with the aid of these streamers plus a series of visual punches in the film which will seem to flutter as they appear. These flutters are the correct mathematical divisions of the bars although he may not necessarily adhere strictly to them. They are his guide. *You,* the music editor, have to figure out where they are going to be and punch them in the film.

We start by breaking down the time value between the beginning and the first anchor point, which is 0:48—48 seconds. Let us say without even looking at the music that *if* this portion were 12 bars of 4/4, it might simply be assumed that each bar is 4 seconds long. But such is not the case—there are 13 bars and moreover there is a 5/4 bar in bar 13 to make the work a little more difficult. We do know that there are 53 beats between these points: 48 for the first 12 bars and 5 beats for bar 13. We must therefore find out how long each quarter note is. We divide the 48 second by 53 quarter notes. This is actually 53 intervals because we are going to the downbeat of the next section, the start of bar 14. When we put 48 ÷ 53 into the calculator, we get 0.9056603 second. This is how long a quarter note is, roughly nine tenths of a second. If we then multiply this by 4 we get 3.6226412 seconds. This is how long a 4/4 bar is. The length of the 5/4 bar, bar 13, would of course be 0.9056603 plus 3.6226412, totaling 4.5283015 seconds.

We now start at bar 1, which is 0:00, and add the value of a 4/4 bar to it; then bar 2 comes at 3.6226412 seconds. We do not need all the places past the decimal but we do need the first place, which indicates tenths. On bar 2 of the music we write 0:03.6 (three and six tenths seconds). We will write only the tenths-place digit on the music but we will add at least three more digits into the calculator to keep our accumulation going or we will fall short at the end. We now add 3.622 to bar 2 which will get us to 7.2446412 (0:07.2) or seven and two tenths seconds. We write this timing on bar 3. We continue this way until the down beat of bar 13, which brings us to 0:43.5. Since this is a 5/4 bar it is longer than any of the first twelve. Not only do we add the 3.622, which is the time for a 4/4 bar, but we also add the 0.905 for the extra quarter note. This brings us to 0:47.9, which is a couple of frames short of 0:48 but for all intents and purposes is perfect. The streamer will be at 0:48.

The reason we fell short by one tenth second is that we are not adding all the numbers to the right of the decimal point. It isn't necessary but if you did add them you would come out right. However, nothing really would be gained doing this.

Three Pages of Music Sketch. Note the streamer marks at 0:00, 0:48, and
1:13.1. Note the punch marks at the start of bars 2, 3, 5, 7, and later.

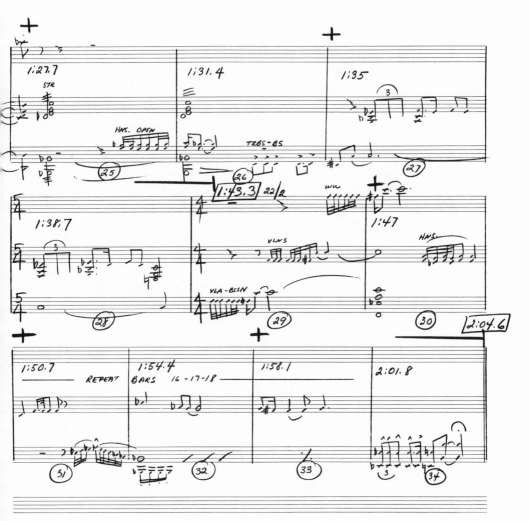

You have now completed the first part of this computation and will proceed to the second part.

Between 0:48, where you just stopped, and the next anchor point of 1:13.1 is 0.25.1. To get this, you enter 73.1 (which is 1:13.1) into the calculator, then subtract 48.0 to get the answer. (One minute cannot be entered into the calculator so it must be converted to 60 seconds. That's why 1:13.1 becomes 73.1). You will also notice that you have a 3/4 bar in bar 20, other bars being 4/4. Hence you now have 27 intervals between the down beat of bar 14 and the next anchor point, which is the down beat of bar 21. You take the total time between these two points, which is 0:25.1, and divide it by 27 intervals, getting .9296296 second for a quarter note. You multiply this by 4 and get 3.7185184 seconds or 0:03.7, which is the value of a 4/4 bar. The value of the 3/4 bar is 2.788888 seconds.

This procedure is done again between anchor points and repeated exactly as with the first section. You do this until you have finished. You will notice that the last section goes only to the last quarter of bar 34, so there are only 23 divisions between points rather than 24.

Should you find that there are no 5/4 or 3/4 bars between sections that are in 4/4, the process is a bit simpler. This means that all the bars are the same, in 4/4 and not intermixed. When you divide to find your interval you will not have to deal in quarter notes but in bars, so simply divide the time by the number of bars since they are all identical.

There is one other thing that could add to the complications. The sketch may call for a ritard in one of the bars. A bar with a ritard would naturally be a little longer. I am referring to a planned ritard. If the conductor found that he was a bit ahead of his flutters he would naturally have to make a slight ritard before his next streamer to catch up. That would be a necessary one, not what we mean here.

We must make a hypothetical case to demonstrate how to allow the extra time needed for this bar with the ritard. Let's say we started to play at bar 1 and played for 10 bars before our streamer on the downbeat of bar 11. The sketch calls for a slight ritard in bar 10. All bars are in 4/4 so this means 40 beats. Bar 10 would require a little more time. Instead of 4 beats in this bar we would allow the time of 4½ beats. You would have to do more than determine the time value of a quarter note. Instead of dividing your time by 40 beats, you would divide it by 40.5, that is, 40 for the 40 quarter notes plus .5 for the extra half beat added in bar 10 to take care of the ritard. Now, to determine the time value of a bar you would multiply by 4 the value you determined for the quarter note. Each of the first 9 bars will be of this value but bar 10 will be of this value *plus* the value of the half beat. This will give bar 10 the extra time needed for the ritard. Analyzing this procedure, you will see how this resembles what you had to do on the sketch in bar 13, which is the 5/4 bar.

After you have done all the computations and all the timings are on the music, you are ready for the next step. You could not have made any mistakes in calculations because if you did you would not have reached your next anchor point at the proper timing, so this work you have done is self correcting.

You are going to indicate on the music which bars are going to be punched. Your sketch is marked with a streamer in the beginning. You will put a flutter punch, as shown in the diagram, on the downbeat of bar 2 and another on the downbeat of bar 3. A "flutter punch" means a series of holes, not one hole only. You will then flutter punch every alternate bar until you get to the next streamer. You will punch the bars after the streamer, bar 15 and bar 16, and again every alternate bar, and so on. Mark a $+$ in red on the sketch in these bars, as the illustration shows. You are now ready for the film work.

Setting the picture on the synchronizer, we set the start of the cue on 0:00. The synchronizer should have a seconds counter. If it doesn't you will have to set the picture up on the Moviola and, using the seconds counter, mark off the frames for punching.

Run through the picture, marking with a $+$ the first frames of the bars that require punches and with a $\bigcirc$ those requiring streamers. Do the whole cue. You are already familiar with the use of the streamer board, so do all the streamers, and the punch at the end of each, throughout the cue. After you have done that you will punch the frames marked with a $+$ for the flutter punches. Punch this frame, then every alternate frame until you have punched a total of five. This will give you 5 punches, one in every alternate frame over 9 frames from the first to the last. (At Twentieth Century-Fox they have a multiple punch made specially to punch a series of 10 holes encompassing 19 frames, but I don't think that many are necessary.)

Continue your punching for all the bars in the cue that require

flutter punches. When you have done all the punching, the whole cue is finished.

You should now check your work on the Moviola. Run the picture while following the sketch and conduct even if you are not the best conductor in the world. You will see the start streamer. You will know the approximate tempo. You will see the flutter when you reach bar 2 and the flutter when you reach bar 3 and the other punch-marked beats. You will not have to look up from the music; the flutters are very obvious. They will show you how accurately you are marking the tempo. If the first flutter comes in too late, you know you are conducting too fast and vice versa. Like you, the conductor can follow his score without looking up at the screen because the flutters almost have the effect of lighting up the score page and in addition they are indicated in red + marks on the music sketch. You *must* put the flutter indications on the conductor's copy of the sketch. Don't forget, this information came from you so it would be up to *you* to see that it is put on his copy. If he should conduct from the score rather than the sketch, you will have to put the flutter marks on the score also. He uses the flutters to control his tempo. It is sort of a visual clock on the screen. He may miss some punches but they are not really important to him as long as he knows where he is in the music in relation to the flutters. He can speed up or slow down as required. He will, however, look up to catch the streamers because they *are* important. After that he will look at the music.

This is the whole Newman system but it takes a great deal of time to prepare for it, as you can now see. Some conditions may arise that are not covered by this explanation. These problems you will have to work out with your own ability and the knowledge at hand.

26 / **Changing the Pitch of a Track**

Changing the pitch of a track would be done only because it becomes necessary to bring something into the proper pitch because it is sharp or flat. (Or because the change will achieve some special effect you are looking for.) There is some very sophisticated electronic equipment on the market today that can alter the pitch of music without changing the length of the recorded material. This pitch-changing equipment has several trade names. It can be obtained by itself; it also comes built into another piece of equipment called a digital delay. It actually does what might have been considered impossible at one time, almost like putting 33 ounces into a 32-ounce bottle without overflowing. I have heard the finished product and it is good. But too much of a change is not recommended; a slight adjustment to correct pitch is acceptable. The change method does have more limitations when used with music than when used with voice or sound effects.

You should experiment with the particular piece of music that you are in need of altering. I have been told by some engineers whose opinion I respect that this kind of change will not always work satisfactorily with every type of music. Fast music will suffer less than slow music during this electronic transposition. I have also been given to understand that it is not advisable to do this change with a piano solo.

When length is not important and there is no synchronization problem, slowing up or accelerating the track will alter the pitch, but

Changes in Film Speeds for Raising or Lowering the Pitch of Music Tracks

(*Bases:* A = 440 cycles per second; percents computed to the nearest tenth; film speeds computed to the nearest whole foot per minute.)

To Raise the Recorded Pitch—Read Up

Change in Musical Steps	Percent	Feet per minute
6 steps. Octave	100.0	180
5½ steps. Major 7th	88.8	170
5 steps. 7th	78.2	160
4½ steps. 6th	68.2	151
4 steps. Augmented 5th	58.7	143
3½ steps. 5th	49.8	135
3 steps. Augmented 4th	41.4	127
2½ steps. 4th	33.5	120
2 steps. Major 3rd	26.0	113
1½ steps. Minor 3rd	18.9	107
1 step. Major 2nd	12.2	101
½ step. Minor 2nd	5.9	95
0 step. Tonic	0.0	90

To Lower the Recorded Pitch—Read Down

Change in Musical Steps	Percent	Feet per minute
0 step. Tonic	0.0	90
½ step. Minor 2nd	5.6	85
1 step. Major 2nd	10.9	80
1½ steps. Minor 3rd	15.9	76
2 steps. Major 3rd	20.6	71
2½ steps. 4th	25.1	67
3 steps. Augmented 4th	29.3	64
3½ steps. 5th	33.3	60
4 steps. Augmented 5th	37.0	57
4½ steps. 6th	40.5	54
5 steps. 7th	43.9	50
5½ steps. Major 7th	47.0	48
6 steps. Octave	50.0	45

it will also affect the overall length. This conversion too should be done with caution. The characteristics of the instruments or voices are bound to change accordingly. You couldn't permit this change with a known vocalist because the change would make him or her sound like a different person. However, if you raise or lower the pitch of an instrument no more than a half tone, the result is not likely to be disturbingly conspicuous except to some very sensitive ears.

Curiosity prompted me to devise the chart on page 116. It shows the different percentage increases and decreases in speed that would be necessary to produce the changes in pitch up or down for a complete octave. Applying this table, unless you are looking for a special effect, won't make you happy from a musical standpoint, but you may find the information interesting.

I once had a guitar track that was off pitch. Before the scene was shot, no one had bothered to check the guitar pitch. The performer himself didn't know it was slightly off. It was not out of tune but just about a quarter of a tone flat. If it were to remain that way without any scoring under it, nothing would have had to be done because no one would ever have known unless he had an ear for absolute pitch. The composer wanted to score the scene leading up to the guitar, then play sustained harmony underneath it, and then continue with additional scoring after the guitar was over. I had to bring the guitar into pitch. I knew this would help the composer. I also knew what a problem this was going to be for me. Had the pitch changer been around at that time it would have been ideal for this situation, but it wasn't. Luckily the greatest portion of this guitar passage was not visual so it helped my problem. Bringing the guitar into pitch is done strictly by ear. I had to speed up the film just enough to correct it, but couldn't find film equipment with a variable speed; professional recording equipment is run by motors with a constant speed, controlled by the frequency of the cycle in the electric supply, which is 60 cycles per second. These motors cannot be controlled by the use of rheostats as a variable-speed motor can. The only way you can change the speed of this equipment is to change the frequency of the power-supply cycle. If you want to speed up a track the power supply would have to be run at a higher frequency, and vice versa. A piece of equipment called a resolver is used for this. It can slow down or speed up the frequency of the cycle and thereby change the speed of the recorder motor. You operate the control in the same way you would operate a rheostat. If you increased the frequency to 65 cycles, the tape would run faster. You would then record to another tape recorder at normal speed and make a standard-speed copy. From this you would make your 35mm prints.

The overall new guitar track that I made did end up a bit short. In the film, the guitarist started to play on scene and finished off scene. I ran the new adjusted track as far as I could get away with it. I couldn't stay on the scene too long and hold sync. The rest of the problem was helped by the picture editor. He did it by cutting away from the scene sooner and never cutting back until the guitar was over. I then retimed the sequence and the final result was beautiful both audibly and visually.

Digital Delay Effects

Earlier in this article I mentioned the digital delay. With this equipment you can put a track through the input and the output can be delayed any amount up to about 600 milli-seconds, which is roughly about 14 frames. This delayed signal, if played together with the original, will produce an echo effect, sounding as though it were played in a large auditorium or through a typical public-address system. Some models have more than one output, allowing still another delay from the first one with its own millisecond control. This enables you to set individually timed delays to affect each signal output. Without equipment like this, the only way you could achieve this effect would be by making additional prints and building them on separate units, staggering them as desired.

27 / Multiple-Track Recordings

Our interest in multiple-track recording is only in its application to motion pictures. The subject can be more exhaustively explained by experts in this field and in books on sound recording. This chapter is not meant to be highly technical.

Multiple-track systems have been around for a long time and are getting more multiple as time goes on. They originated with the commercial record studios. At their inception they were never used for motion-picture scoring. They started as low as four tracks on ½-inch tape; I don't dare say how high the multiple track goes now, but at this writing I am personally familiar with the 24-track machine. This may be antiquated equipment when this book comes to print.

One picture I worked on, *American Hot Wax,* included a rock concert for which the musical numbers were recorded on 48 tracks by using two synchronized 24-track machines.

For a good deal of the musical effects and gimmickry used today, multiple-track recording has numerous advantages. It allows for expansion not possible before. Addition, elimination, or replacement of instrumentalists or vocalists is as simple as pushing buttons. Audio effects and experimentation become endless.

Another purpose that the multiple-track method serves is that when you record, whether for motion pictures or for commercials, you don't have to worry too much about balance as long as the rendition of the orchestra is on the tape. You don't have to pay an expensive orchestra to record take after take because the mixer is not happy with the balance. With all the microphones he has strung up, it's amazing he keeps his sanity at times. The object is to get a good rendition laid down on the multiple track.

With practically every musician on his own channel, the mixer can balance and rebalance endlessly with the multiple track after the orchestra has been dismissed. Doing this is a lot less expensive than making takes. Not only are most of the musicians in isolation on their own channel but a few channels might be used for one musician alone, especially the percussionist whose instrumental spread can take up quite a bit of floor space.

When I worked on the picture *First Love* with John Barry, we recorded on sixteen track but mixed down to three track simultaneously. This combination did have a few drawbacks because the mixer had more to worry about—trying to concentrate on a three-track mix while recording his sixteen track. It turned out that a few of the cues had to be dubbed down again because when we got on the dubbing stage it was necessary to bring out an instrument for which there was no control on the three track. The cue had to be redubbed with a new balance. This experience demonstrates a valuable advantage of multiple-track recording.

Noise-Reduction Systems

The names Dolby and DBX should be mentioned in connection with multiple-track recording. These two different systems work in conjunction with multiple-track recording. Some musical purists are not in favor of using them but beyond doubt they are here to stay. Either of them reduces background noise to an absolute minimum and they are particularly advantageous when recording multiple tracks. The reasoning is that when you record multiple tracks, the result is the same as that from recording many individual tapes simultaneously. If you were then to play a number of these individual tapes back synchronously, there would be an equal number of tape hisses, one for each track, even though very slight. Combining these tapes compounds the hiss. These noise-reduction systems tend to lower the background hiss, thereby increasing the signal-to-noise ratio. When a track is recorded with either of these systems, it is said to be encoded. In the final dubdown to a 35mm print for dubbing it must be decoded. It is possible, though, to record your multiple track, dub it down and go to final dubbing with encoded tracks but they will be decoded while dubbing.

With regard to intercutting on 35mm, do not attempt to intercut a decoded track with an encoded track. They must be edited into separate units. You must be aware of what you have, as the difference between the two may not be sufficiently obvious on the Moviola. Also remember that the Dolby and DBX systems are not compatible—not any more than either one is with a decoded track.

28 / On the Scoring Stage

The composer has his big day when his score comes to life on the scoring stage. The producer and the director will probably be there to see and hear the scored music for the first time. You—the music editor—will have distributed copies of the scoring logs to all concerned. The recording sequence of the cues will not be in the sequence of the picture. The recording sessions will be set up by the music department, which plans the sessions according to the size of the orchestra. This scheduling is done for economic reasons, naturally. If the scoring requires a few sessions, the first session may use the largest group. The second session may be smaller. If you go another day, there may be just a small group for source music.

Once, in a rare instance, we were scoring a picture on the same day that we started dubbing. The cues had to be recorded in proper continuity regardless of the orchestra breakdown. I had to have someone else cut them into the dubbing units just as soon as they were recorded and sent directly to the dubbing stage. This was an exception and certainly not the rule.

You should have a convenient seat where you can handle the time clock and the digital metronome and where you and the composer can see and hear each other. You will probably get into a few huddles with him before the session is over. He may want to discuss some things with you and vice versa. Neither of you want the whole orchestra to hear your conversation. One thing you should have available is your calculator. You will find this very handy on the stage. You also must have your book of cues and be ready for the downbeat. The orchestra breakdown chart (see page 97) prepared by the music department will give you the recording sequence, so without anyone asking you, you will set the digital metronome to the tempo of the first cue. The conductor will start to rehearse and will ask you to run the click for the tempo. Whenever he is ready to start recording, be sure the click is turned off. The automatic start will take over if you are using this method. If you are using the manual start, the blue streamer will be your indication to push the start button for the warning clicks. It is good to follow the score and kill the clicks at the end, probably where the fermata starts. Doing this is a good idea because occasionally the click has been known to leak from the musicians' headphones and be heard on the track. It would probably never be noticed while the music is playing but might be heard at the end during a sustained chord. The conductor would also like to hear the click stopped when he reaches the chord at the end, whether it is sustained or cut off.

There may be times when the conductor will tell you that he would like to change the click. He would like to repeat two bars of music in the same sequence but doesn't know at what tempo to play it. You have to do some quick calculation. Say for instance the cue has 85 bars and ends on the downbeat of bar 86. Adding two additional bars means that if he wants to end in the same place, it would now be the downbeat of bar 88 and that means the cue would have to go a bit faster.

Let's say that you were playing it originally at a 15/5 (15.675), 2 beats to the bar. That means that you had a total of 171 beats or 170 intervals. You now want to add 2 more bars, which is 4 more clicks because you are in 2 beats to the bar. You will now have 174 intervals instead of 170. Go back to the beginning. Put the 170 intervals in the calculator and multiply 170 by 15.625. This was your original tempo and you have to determine how many frames there are to the entire cue. You get an answer of 2656.25. The .25 is only one quarter of a frame. You can leave it in the calculator. This is the total number of frames in the cue from start to finish. You must now divide it by 174, the new number of intervals you want, which is 175 beats. Divide the 2656.25 by 174 and you will get the answer of 15.265804. This is the new click tempo to give the added 2 bars within the same time. What kind of a tempo is 15.265804? As close as you can see, it is a 15/2 because what follows after the decimal point (.265804) is just about the same as .250, which is two eighths. Your tempo then is a 15/2 and the composer has his two extra bars. Naturally, the longer the sequence, the less noticeable the tempo difference because the change is infinitesimal over all these beats. All this that took paragraphs to explain and describe actually takes less than one minute to do on the stage. This new tempo will get to within just a few frames of the end of the cue and that is close enough. This may all seem a frightening job to do on the scoring stage, but if you practice by making up a few hypothetical changes on your own, you'll see how quickly you can do it. The request for a change could be in reverse, that is, to take out a bar or two, which would make the new tempo a bit slower rather than faster. That operation wouldn't change the method.

The composer may want an additional streamer here and there that he didn't ask for originally, so make it a practice to keep the streamer board and the punch in the projection booth during a scoring session.

You will be keeping records of all the selected takes and of any intercutting to be done. You might have a cue with long pauses between music phrases. Sometimes it is difficult to have complete quiet during these pauses. There may be a chair squeak, or someone may accidentally hit something. If you notice some particular noise during pauses, make a note of this. This noise does not make the take unusable as long as there is no music there, but you must remember to remove any extraneous noises and replace the footage with plain leader when building your units for dubbing. You may not always hear unnecessary sounds in these silent sections during the recording because of where you will be sitting and because of the multiple microphones. It is best to play the print on the Moviola and check each channel. If you are working with a single-stripe head on the Moviola, you will have to run through each section channel by channel, shifting the head after each run through. A sound could be noticeable on one channel and never be heard on another.

29 / **After the Scoring**

When the scoring session is over it is up to the music editor to get the prints, break them down from the full rolls, and build the units for dubbing. If there were any playbacks or production source cues, everything relating to them should be already assembled and cut in, except possibly for some sweetening done at the scoring. You may have many tracks built at this time. The only thing left to do is to cut the scoring in. If nothing has been built, then you start from scratch. If you have an assistant to break down the prints, that's fine. If not you'll have to do this also. Not all assignments will afford you the luxury of an assistant.

If you scored to sixteen tracks, only the selected takes will have been dubbed down to 35mm. If you scored to 35mm you will have a lot to break down because the NG (no good, rejected, unsatisfactory) takes and the false starts will also be in the rolls. Just set all this footage aside. You won't need it, but don't throw anything away.

During some spare time previous to this, you should have prepared all your music units with head leaders and start marks so that you can start right in editing.

The picture should be set up on the Moviola with the footage counter set at 0000. The music units should be set up on the bench with the synchronizer counter also set at 0000. The dubbing logs should be handy to write up as you progress with the editing. Your music prints should be set up in sequence on the shelves of the cutting bench. Now you are ready to proceed.

Taking each cue in turn, run them all with the picture to be sure everything is as you have seen it on the scoring stage. Especially if you scored without projection, then you most certainly had better run everything with the picture since you did not see it on the scoring stage.

Put sync marks on so that you can cut each piece of music into the units on the bench corresponding to the footage on the Moviola counter. You needn't make your splice more than a half foot before the music starts. Make sure the tails are clean; sometimes a voice will come in after the music is over or a musician will put down his instrument with a clunk.

In exceptional situations, I have cut an entire film on the bench without running it on the Moviola because I knew the synchronization was all right. Having heard the cues with the picture on the scoring stage, and knowing then that the sync was fine, I didn't feel the necessity to go through them again on the Moviola. I needed only to be sure that any excess, before the music started or after it ended, was cut off. Be sure you are right if you attempt to do this.

When you have cues that overlap, cut them on separate tracks. Do not try to intercut them on the same unit. Here is why: You may record a cue that has been broken up in sections for various reasons. The cue will play, and at the end of the section the conductor might have the orchestra play the first downbeat of the following section for smoothness and then make a cut off. An experienced film conductor will do this anyhow. When the next section is recorded, it starts on the downbeat of the new section. Technically, you could cut off the last chord of the previous section (the overlap chord) and replace it with the start of the new section. Here is what happens when you do that: The beginning chord of the new section is musically the same as the overlapping chord recorded on the previous section but it lacks the overtone of what preceded it. If you make a direct cut at the start, it will not sound as good as having both chords hit simultaneously on separate tracks. This latter will sound more natural.

If you have any special reason for wanting to join the outgoing section to the new section on one track, you can. To do this, though, the music should be recorded differently. Section one should still be recorded ending with the downbeat of the new section as before. But the new incoming section should not start cold with the beginning, as before. The recording should start at least a bar before where you intend to make the cut. This overlap will give the necessary overtones at the splice. Be aware of this intention before you get into the scoring session.

If you have any intercutting between different takes of the same cue, make certain that the levels are the same or do not put them on the same track; if the levels are different you will have to split the cue on separate tracks.

If you have planned any intercutting on the scoring stage, treat it now the same way as you would with a cue broken up in sections. If the conductor says he wants to use bar forty to the end from another take, you can split it up or you can intercut it. At the point where you will intercut it, overlap the takes so the previous music's overtones will be on both tracks.

When you are building your dubbing units, a situation may arise whereby you have to clip the end of a cue and it will sound cut off. You may have had to open a cue to insert a short fill; this interruption would cause dropping out of the natural background of the orchestra. The dubbing mixer can remedy this loss if you will indicate to him to use the reverberation chamber at this point. The chamber will carry the outgoing note over through the fill.

When building any music unit in which there is a piece of music that starts on the first frame of the reel, there is something else to consider. On all B reels (even-numbered reels) you can start your music on the first frame of picture, which is at 12 feet. You must also use a second print of the music, which will start on the first frame of leader after the picture on the outgoing A reel. This second print is used because of the joining of the reels by the laboratory. This music must also be dubbed on the outgoing reel and will therefore be dubbed in both places. You do not have to play more than a few feet of the cue on the outgoing reel but if you have the room you can leave the entire print intact.

It is not advisable to start a cue on the first frame of picture on an A reel (odd-numbered reel). This is at a projection machine change-over and during this process you may not have a clean entrance on the music. This is the human element at work. The projectionist uses a visual guide to make this change. It is therefore preferable to delay your music start at least twenty frames at the head of an A reel.

Another method is used that eliminates the duplicate music print on the outgoing reel. It is called a pull-up. After the entire show is dubbed, the dubbing mixer makes a transfer of the dubbed master at the head of each reel. This has all three elements of the dubbed sound—voices, sound effects, and music. Only the opening few feet of each reel is needed. This transfer print is spliced on the dubbed master at the end of each previous reel so that all the sound is duplicated in both places. This process is usually taken care of by the sound-effects editor.

If any humming or whistling is in the film editor's dialogue track, it should be removed and edited into one of your music units. Whether it is in the dialogue track or the music track will not have any effect on the domestic dubbing, but can cause problems in dubbing for foreign languages, should there be any. The humming or whistling should be integrated into the music stripe.

Final dubbing is usually recorded on a three-stripe master: one stripe for music, one stripe for sound effects, and one stripe for dialogue and/or narration. The dubbing panel allows the dubbing mixer the facility to select whichever of these three stripes he prefers for recording any combination of the tracks supplied to him. He would naturally channel the film editor's dialogue track into the dialogue/narration stripe.

But when and if a foreign version is made of the film, it will be made using only two of these three stripes—the stripe of the sound effects and the stripe of the music; the foreign language will go on a new dialogue track that will supplant the original. Each of the three stripes on the master is isolated. New voices will be recorded and the film will then be redubbed, using the new foreign voice track together with the domestic sound-effects and music stripes. If the humming or whistling were left on the picture editor's dialogue track it would not get recorded in the foreign version of the film. To avoid its being lost, it should be on the music stripe.

Singing presents a different problem. I am not referring to someone singing "La-la-la" but to the singing of actual words. This editing should be discussed with the producer or director before you build your dubbing units, so you may know how they intend to handle the song. In some pictures the nature of the song might call for a translation, in which event the vocal would go on the dialogue/narration stripe and neither the original vocal nor the translated vocal would be heard on the music stripe.

But if the picture is a musical featuring vocal stars, the vocal does belong on the music track. Anyone who goes to the theater to see a Barbra Streisand film, for instance, goes to hear *her* voice, not to hear her vocal as redone by someone else in a foreign language. Accordingly her vocal is integrated in the music stripe and must not be removed to leave only the orchestra to accompany the other voice in the other language.

Source music is very often edited differently from scoring. It might be said that the music comes in "in progress" at the beginning and goes out "in progress" at the end. This means that when you cut to a scene in which source music is heard, as in a restaurant, the music is assumed to have been playing previously. Observers are coming in at that chance point. It may be anywhere in the music and not necessarily at the beginning. The same applies to the end: the scene may be cutting away while the music is still playing. The entrance or the exit of the music in progress doesn't always sound good, but the effect in cutting off the music abruptly is meant to add to the feeling of being "in progress." If you had a cut to a restaurant and started the source cue at the beginning of the track with the beginning of a scene, the feeling would be completely different.

The "in progress" cuts are also very effective in another way. Assume you have a restaurant scene and that the music is playing. After a minute or so you have a scene cut to *later* in the same restaurant, or even *another* restaurant. The music would inevitably not be the same. You are therefore cutting from one cue to another cue with no break inbetween. The latter piece might even be a different tempo. The jarring effect of the music cut between these two pieces has added considerably in telling you that the action is later, or even somewhere else.

Cutting into a source cue in progress doesn't mean to just cut in anywhere. It does mean not to come in at the beginning. Try to at least make an entrance between notes rather than during notes. When you have made your decision as to how you are going to cut the source music at the beginning of a scene, you have also made your decision how to take it out at the end—it must necessarily go out wherever you cut away. You may not particularly like the resulting cut at the end; then you do have a little choice: shift it a bit to make the end sound good and let the start come wherever it comes. I have always felt that the cut away should be the better sound than the cut to, if they can't both be good. A bad cut away jars me more than a bad entrance.

Source music may at times be on the left channel only. If your source music is on a stripe, then there is no question about it being the left channel. This means that the beginning and the end of the cue that is not used can remain on the reel but it must be flopped. That is, the unused portion of the music will be spliced to the used portion upside down. The unused portion will be lying on the right-channel side, but since this unit is running on the left channel, only the used part will be heard.

There is one advantage to this method of flopping, both to the music editor and to the director. This advantage can come about on the dubbing stage. Suppose you were using about one minute of a source cue that was considerably longer than needed. You had cut it in the reel to cover a scene and had flopped both ends because it was to come in and go out in progress. You have the entire cue built into the music unit but you hear only the portion you have chosen, which is positioned on the left channel. Several things could happen at the dubbing session that can be fixed very quickly with flopped sections. In one case the director might say: "Let's hear the source outside before we cut inside." You have the unused portions of the source music right there in the reel; they are merely acting as blank leader or spacer by being flopped. You can then unflop as much as you need and it will join with the cut previously made—still in progress. Also, if you should want to have the source continue longer at the end, you would do the same as you did at the beginning, only in reverse.

To imagine another case, the director just may not like the portion of the source music *you* chose to cut in. You can easily alter the situation with flopping, shifting, and unflopping. If your source music were on a three track, the head and tail trims would probably be somewhere in the cutting room, since this cannot be flopped for mechanical reasons.

Regardless of the "in progress" cutting of source music, there is still another way that it can be edited. Take for an example a long scene at a party. Music is being played almost continuously but we do not stay in the room with this music throughout. We may have many cuts to the exterior or to an adjacent room and then back to the interior. It is natural that if we are close enough to the source when we cut away, it will still be heard but not at the same volume. The best way to edit this, both to make it easier for the mixer and also to make it sound better, is to split your source on two tracks. This will enable you to have one unit for the interior and one for the exterior, which will be set at a lower volume level. The dubbing mixer doesn't have to go crazy raising and lowering his levels to accommodate the situation. They can be preset. Situations could exist where you would have source music on three tracks, each one with its own volume setting for different distances.

When you are cutting your source-music track with this method, there should be an overlap of one sprocket between the tracks. If the cue starts on the interior, run it until the cut to the exterior. Make the splice one sprocket after the cut. The part that you cut off, which is for the exterior, starts on the scene cut on the other track. This means that you have overlapped one sprocket. You are actually losing a sprocket every time you cut between the two tracks.

This method of cutting source music for perspective has one disadvantage as opposed to just laying in the entire cue on one track. If there is a decision to move the cue for any reason, it will be impossible without putting the whole cue back together again and starting all over. If you intend to do this type of editing, discuss it with the director so that he understands. Let him know that doing this type of editing makes for very smooth segues from interior to exterior and also have him understand why it will cause trouble if he makes a sudden decision to shift the source music. Have him come to the cutting room and view the picture with the source music. When he is satisfied with its placement then you can split it between tracks. In my experience a director has seldom cared about the actual position of the source music but I wouldn't go to the trouble of splitting it without consulting him.

Of course, the easiest way is to put the source music on one track and just cue the picture for the different volume levels. It is usually done this way but I prefer the other.

Another reason for splitting a source cue on two tracks is as follows: During a source-music sequence, someone makes a phone call. When you cut to the person answering, not only might you hear the futzed voice in the receiver as the person is listening, but the director might also want the audience to hear the source music. This source music would also have to be futzed since it's coming from the same place as the voice. If the director doesn't want music heard in the receiver, it is easy to drop because you have already split it up.

Futzing is an expression used in motion pictures. It is the compression of sound at both ends of the audio spectrum, removing the high and low frequencies. It is a form of distortion but a very useful one, for with it a track can be made to sound like the quality that would come from the telephone earpiece. Futzing is also used for representing small transistor radios because of the tiny speakers. Anytime you have a car radio in a scene, whether it is playing music or voice, it should always be set up for futzing. When you have any sound at all that has to be done this way, cut it into a unit of its own so that the mixer can preset his equalizer. It is all right to cut it into a regular unit as long as you have plenty of space between it and any other track that is to play normally. Don't make it impossible for the mixer to handle.

31 / **Cutting In Cues between Reels**

Cues between A to B reels (odd to even numbered reels) can be continuous music. Theater-release prints are on 2000-foot reels. This combining is done by the laboratory after dubbing. Reels one and two will be combined, reels three and four will be combined, and so on.

Even though you may have timed a cue between reels at a machine changeover such as 2M5/3M1, it should have been written with the proper pause so that one print can be used for both reels when cutting in the cue for dubbing. If the cue was 1M6/2M1 for instance (no changeover), then two prints should be ordered. In dubbing, the music can continue past the end of the A reel. When cutting in the part for 1M6, you can run it as far past the end of the reel as you like if it doesn't make the reel too oversized.

Line up both of your copies of 1M6/2M1 in perfect sync to each other on the synchronizer. Run these down in sync with the picture. At the end of the reel, where the picture joins the end leader, mark this frame line on both prints. Be very cautious when using two prints. Don't ever take for granted that they are in perfect sync. After marking off these two lines at the end of the reel, listen to both prints at this point. Be certain that the modulations are identical at the lines. It has happened by accident that both prints were not in perfect sync even though it is never expected to happen. If you find this to be the case, then readjust slightly where the reels join to make the music in perfect sync. Leave the outgoing print as it is. If any slight adjustment

133

Glen Glenn Sound
6624 Romaine Street, Hollywood, California 90038
Telephone (213) 469-7221

FIRST LOVE
Reel 5 Music

MUSIC 1
3 track

246 5M1
L – Brass
C – Perc. W.W.
R – Strings

378 5M2
3 track

378

502

540 5M3

580 5M4

580

746

790 5M5/6M1

805 Cont'd in Rl.6

MUSIC 3
Stripe

378 Guitar
Sweetener
(Left)only

502

MUSIC 4
3 track

540 Alternate for
5M3

580

Same instrument breakdown
for all tracks.

A Portion of a Dubbing Log

has to be made, do it on the incoming print. You can cut your print into the outgoing reel regardless. This will not change. Give yourself a new sync mark and use *this* to be cut in at the head of the incoming reel. The music at these two marks must match. When the prints are joined after dubbing, it will be perfect.

Here is what can happen if you do not check your marks on both prints by listening to them. You cannot know, while you are listening on the dubbing stage, that they are not in perfect sync. No one else will know either—but when the reels are joined at the laboratory the discrepancy will show up and we don't want it to get that far. Discovery then could only mean redubbing to fix the trouble.

When all your units are edited and the dubbing logs are complete, everything is ready to go to the dubbing stage.

Page 134 shows a sample of a dubbing log. Notice that when a three track is put on the log, the channel breakdown of the orchestra is given for the mixer.

32 / Tracking

There is so much to know about the phase of work called tracking that it could fill a book of its own. What does tracking mean? It
means selecting and editing a piece of music for a sequence to replace
the piece that was written for it originally. It means selecting and editing a piece of music for a sequence for which nothing was written at
all. It means using the music that *was* written for the sequence but altering it in some way so that it is not the same as before.

Years ago, when some studios finished a picture, they would track
the entire picture with a temporary score from their own music library. They would do a quick dubbing and send it out for a preview.
After the preview, the regular procedure of scoring would start.
Using the temporary score was a way of getting a reaction on the picture quickly. The music came from pictures scored by many composers; much of it may have come from the composer who was going
to do the score after the preview.

In such work, the music editor practically becomes the composer
since he adapts a score of library music to fit the picture. There have
been times when the tracked score was so good that it was better than
the score finally written for the picture. And why not? Just because a
composer writes an original score does not mean that his judgment is
any better than that of the person selecting music from a library, or
even as good. Also, the music editor has much to select from. He can
run the sequences with many different tracks to find the one best

suited. The composer generally does not bring in an alternate score. He can't come in with more than he has written for the picture and what he brings in is what the music editor has to use.

This practice is not used today but a good deal of tracking is done in features every day in the week. This applies to television also. This tracking is different in that the cues used in it come from the score itself. The recorded score will not always just lay in as it was recorded. If, after a recording session, some music is wanted for a sequence that was never scored, it has to come from the music that *was* scored. It must then be tailored by the music editor to fit the sequence. You may have to lengthen or shorten the cues selected.

Some independent feature films do not have any scores written for them at all. There are music libraries that have just about everything you could want to score a picture with. They charge a flat license fee for the unlimited use of all the music they have in their library. The music that these libraries have has been written especially for this purpose. I am not going to compare this library music to an original score in any way because undoubtedly the music in the library has been used many times over. For the independent producer of a low-budget film there are some advantages. Cost heads the list.

This would be the procedure on one of these films. After spotting it with the producer and the editor, the music editor would go to one of these libraries and select all the music cues from records. These are not commercial records. They are discs of the cues made for selection purposes only. Then you would have the producer come to this place where the selection was done and you would play each cue for him, telling him what each cue is for. He would be able to visualize, except for the final editing, how the cue would be for each sequence. If he didn't like anything in particular, he could select something else right then and there. After this, you could order your 35mm prints as needed. The final prints you order for cutting are made from the master tape, not from the discs. The next time the producer would hear the music would most likely be on the dubbing stage, but he would have no great surprises, having heard all the music before. Hopefully, you should surprise him with some skillful editing. This is a very enjoyable phase of work but a lot harder than just timing and laying in a score. It could really be called creative music editing.

There is another method of scoring a film inbetween tracking from a library and actual scoring. It also is a low-budget method. The composer may have made a package deal and must make the most of his allotted money. He will score cues for the picture but not necessarily to timings. He may not have received any timings at all but he will write enough material to track the picture. To do this will take careful planning. The music editor must make sure that the composer has covered everything needed. He may have provided a theme set or two for the different characters in the picture. He may or may not work with you when you start editing. If you have worked out what you need very thoroughly, you can track an excellent score.

Tracking does require skill. I am not referring just to the tailoring of cues by shortening and lengthening. I am referring to the ability to know what to use for any given sequence. Making these choices is like what the composer has to do except that he has to write it. The similarity is that either the composer or the music editor must think "How do I want to treat this sequence? What mood do I want?" What you select shows your dramatic ability to score even though you are not a composer. Not every composer has this dramatic ability. It is the ability that separates a film composer from others who would like to be so called.

Tracking in some forms is *very* creative. All the textbooks in the world cannot teach creative tracking. When you have to decide which music is right for which scene, only your own sense of dramatics can tell you. I am sure that many times while you were watching a television show you have said to yourself, "That music doesn't seem right." The composer's or editor's choice must not have been the best or it couldn't have given you that impression. I make no attempt to try to explain what is right when it comes to selecting music. It cannot be done by explanation. I will only try to explain some of the mechanical techniques in tracking.

For tracking, you should be using a Moviola with two sound heads. The photograph on page 22 shows this type. The dialogue track must be kept on the outside head. If it were kept on the inside head you could not run any music wild on the outside head. The motor does not power this head. The motor powers the inside head only and drives all three when they are interlocked. What you must do is to leave the inside head free to run the music. You must also remember that every time you want to run a piece of music, you must disengage *both* interlocks. When you want to run the dialogue with the picture, you must engage *both* interlocks. If you forget to engage either, your picture will run out of sync with your dialogue. You will get into the habit of attending properly to interlocks and will do it without even thinking about it. That is the operational procedure.

When you are trying to fit a piece of music to any sequence, the chances are that the first thing you will do is to set the beginning of the music on the beginning of the sequence and run it. It will most probably be too long as you would not be likely to have chosen something too short for what you need. You will then have to shorten it. If the piece you selected turns out to be too short, don't let the length discourage you. The proper selection is more important than its length, and you can always lengthen it by repeating whatever bars are necessary to make it fit. The actual editing is a matter of opinion. No two editors are likely to do the same thing with the same piece of music.

Always try to use the natural end of the track rather than just laying in a piece of music and having the mixer fade it out. (I wouldn't even call this tracking.) Let's say that you are going to have to cut a required amount of footage out of a track. Anywhere would be better than the very beginning or the very end. If it is an overall mood cue, it really doesn't make any difference where you cut inbetween.

Two hints are offered on the assumption that the edit is not a perfect one. If it is, then there is no need to cover up anything. If there is dialogue in the scene, try to make your edit fall under the dialogue rather than have the music be in the open—especially if you feel the edit is not the best. Another little trick that helps is this: try to make the edit fall on a scene cut if at all possible. This placing can take away some of its noticeability.

Most scoring ends with a fermata (sometimes called a bird's eye). It is a sustained last note. This will help in not restricting you to exact lengths but will give you quite a bit of leeway in editing.

Another way to approach editing a piece of music is to lay it in from the end and back it up. See what it looks like at the point where you have to come in with it. You might find a very good starting phrase to come in on, even if you have to slide the track a bit from where you laid it in. This way you will not have made any edits, good or bad.

33 / Library of Musical Effects

A library of musical effects can come in very handy. You can build up a library yourself from the recording sessions you attend. Most of the musical effects you would acquire would come from the percussionist—cymbals, tympani, bell trees, and the like. Percussion effects are probably the only form of music that one can use without being concerned about plagiarism. Many effects like these can be used as sweeteners.

A few years ago I did a commercial where the only music used came from a library of musical effects. They were used to accent numerous visual actions and there were about twenty in a 1-minute commercial. There was no recording of any other music for the commercial. The producer was happy. He didn't have to pay for any musicians. What I gave him is not a substitute for music but it was all the particular commercial needed.

You can collect many unusual and rare musical effects over the years. I once managed to obtain a set of orchestral dramatic stings in all twelve tones. These can be superimposed on any music to emphasize a scene cut or action. The way to do it is to first determine the tone being played at the point in question on the music track. Then use the required tonality sting superimposed on another track. It is very effective. I also have the entire range of percussionist's chimes recorded individually and properly slated for each note. In one picture the director didn't feel he was getting what he wanted in one particular cue. It was supposed to have a religious feeling but didn't quite make it. Luckily I happened to have just what the cue needed. It made the cue play much better: on the down beat of each bar I cut chime notes musically correct to each chord. The chimes added the church flavor that was needed.

Every time you get involved in a recording session, make it your business to get something to add to your library. I even managed to have a string section do something for me when there was about ten minutes left in the scoring session. They recorded string tremolos in unison in all twelve tones. Each was about ten seconds long. These can be used for that extra length needed to lead into a cue or to extend at the end of a cue. Your own imagination is your only limit.

34 / The Dubbing Stage

This is where it all comes together.

After the scoring or tracking, if everything went smoothly and the director is not one to make many changes on the dubbing stage (although I've yet to meet one who is not), your part in the dubbing operation is not much more than sitting and relaxing. Dubbing methods have improved tremendously over the years. At one time it was necessary to rehearse many times and reload after each running of the reel. Our modern methods, which some have appropriately named rock and roll, have taken over. The picture and all tracks can stop, reverse, and continue forward, making changes in the dub bit by bit until a perfect dub is achieved. The same section can be done over and over.

The only time the music editor should have anything to do at a dubbing session would be when the director wants to move a cue, add one, delete one, or whatever. In this event you may have to do some tracking. There may be some sequences with no music and the director will decide that he wants some there. The composer will probably not be at the dubbing and you may not be able to reach him on the spur of the moment for any advice. But you should have become pretty familiar with the score, familiar enough to be able to find another cue suitable for tracking the sequence. This could be fun if you are given the time and the other people decide to go to another reel. If they are waiting for you, you could feel the atmosphere limiting your artistic skill.

Make it a habit during the scoring session to take down a quick descriptive record of all the cues, as if for a little library. If then at the dubbing a piece of music is called for to track a sequence, you don't have to start looking through everything trying to remember what each cue sounded like. You can quickly order a reprint from your little description.

You should manage to run the final dub to check that everything that was cut in was used. Some cues may be taken out sooner than indicated on the dubbing logs. Try to get the footages while dubbing. Some cues may also be brought in later than indicated. It isn't always possible to be on the dubbing stage constantly and you can never be sure of what the other people have done. So run that check after the final dub to make sure you have the information you will need later for your legal forms.

35 / **The Preview and After**

Some pictures are not previewed but about half of those that I worked on were. The company wanted me to stay until after the preview in case there were any changes. There always are changes.

When the picture comes back from preview, it should be recoded with a new set of numbers. Such recoding is sometimes skipped, but if the changes are considerable, then it should be done. All your music units should be coded with new numbers, and so should the three-stripe dubbed master. So should the sound-effects units, but these are not the music editor's concern. The picture naturally must be re-coded. The film editor will then make whatever changes there are before turning it back over to the sound-effects editor and the music editor. The sound-effects editor will try to use as much of the three-stripe master as possible; the more that can be used intact, the easier the redubbing. He will resync this unit. You will be able to determine by the coding whether any of the music cues have been affected. Even though there may be many changes in the picture, entire music cues may be untouched.

When you prepare your new dubbing log for the stage, indicate on the sheets if the mixer can use the music on the master or if he must go back to the original units. He may be able to use the three-stripe master for an entire cue, even for a very long one. The extreme tail of the cue may have been cut off because the editor had cut a scene out at that point. The original music unit could be used just to redo this tail of the cue after you resync it. This treatment is easier than a complete redub from the head of the cue.

You might have a reasonable amount of tracking to do. The code numbers will be your guide but you must also use common sense. As an example, a few feet may have been cut from a scene during a music cue, but you may not have to remove any music from the cue at all. The cue can be redubbed from the original unit and can start in the same place where it did originally. It can play in its entirety and end a few feet further in the reel than it did before. This later ending probably will make no difference at all, particularly if the scene went out with a long tail. Or the cue may just be an overall mood cue and it may look just as good even if you have to remove some footage.

There is also a good chance that after the preview the readjusted three-stripe master will be able to handle all your problems and no music cuts will be made. But your original units should be re-synchronized anyhow and sent to the dubbing stage in case they're needed for anything.

36 / Legal Clearance Form

At the conclusion of the dubbing, the music editor's assignment is not over. You still have one last obligation to perform. This is for the legal department of the company you are working for. If you are with a small independent company and there is no specifically identified legal department, someone at the head should nevertheless be supplied with the information described below. Unless this is done, then rest assured that you will receive a call about these matters sometime in the near future.

Every individual piece of music in the picture must be listed on a form that shows the continuity of the music from the first piece to the last. A page of such a form is illustrated. You can make up any form you like to show the necessary information. It must show the composer of each cue and the timing of each. How each piece is used must be indicated (whether it is a vocal or an instrumental, visual or background). Each cue must also have a title. The picture may have had a source music cue or two by some other composer and lyricist. Performance rights may have to be paid to publishers and composers other than the composer of the score. Recording artists may be involved also. If the actual record is used and not just the material, the musicians on that recording will most likely be paid also. If much foreign material (music that did not come from the composer of the score) is used, putting this information together can get very involved. Many selections that are so-called public domain are not always en-

MUSIC CONTINUITY

title **THE VOYAGE OF THE DAMNED** prod. by **TRANSCONTINENTAL FILMS PROD. LTD.** date **AUG. 18, 1976**

CUE #	TITLE OF COMPOSITION	TIMING	INSTR.	BKGD.	VOCAL	VISUAL	COMPOSER	PUBLISHER
1M1	Main Title Part 1	1:05	X	X			Lalo Schifrin	
1M2	Main Title Part 2	1:24	X	X			"	
1M3	Artists Life	3:05	X	X			Johann Strauss	Public Domain
2M1	The House Painter March	1:50	X			X	Lalo Schifrin	Public Domain
2M2	Deutschland Uber Alles	1:30	X			X	Joseph Haydn	Public Domain
2M3	Tales of the Vienna Woods	0:56	X			X	Johann Strauss	Public Domain
2M4	I've Lost My Heart in Budapest	0:48	X			X	Erdelyi Mihaly	Francis Day & Hunter
3M1	Society Rhumba	1:13	X			X	Lalo Schifrin	
3M2	I Can't Give You Anything	1:30	X			X	Jimmy McHugh	Lawrence Wright
3M3	Lovers and Children	2:22	X	X			Lalo Schifrin	
4M1	Hotel Nacional	2:14	X			X	"	
5M1	Perfidia	3:00	X			X	Alberto Dominguez	Southern Pub. Co.
5M2	What's Past is Past	1:31	X	X			Lalo Schifrin	
6M1	Siboney	1:27	X			X	Ernesto Lecuona	Francis Day & Hunter
6M2	An Affirmation of Love	1:11	X	X			Lalo Schifrin	
6M3	Peanut Vendor Song	2:30	X			X	Moises Simons	Lawrence Wright
7M1	Moonlight Serenade	3:37	X			X	Glenn Miller	Big Three Music
7M2	Blue Moon	1:10	X			X	Richard Rodgers	Robbins Music Co.
8M1	Frenesi	0:44				X	Alberto Dominguez	Southern Music Co.
8M2	Vienna Dreams	1:37	X		X	X	Rudolf Sieczynski	Chappell Music
8M3	Dining Room Conga	0:47	X			X	Lalo Schifrin	
8M4	Denise	1:43	X	X			"	

Milton Lustig

The First Page of a Music Continuity. This is a form in which information concerning musical property is recorded for report to the company's legal department.

tirely public. They might be public domain in the United States, Canada, Italy, and France but not in England. The protection laws regarding music are very complicated.

The obligation of supplying this information is all that is expected of the music editor. The legal experts will take care of getting the clearances and making the payments.

After the dubbing you should manage to run the picture and check the time of every cue. Don't depend on the dubbing logs you prepared. If the picture is going to be previewed and come back for changes, then wait until after the second dubbing to do this work.

If you tracked the music from a commercial library, the library people would receive this information from you.

Page 147 shows a sample of the first page of a music continuity made after a final dubbing.

Appendixes

Conversions of Film Dimensions

To Convert	To	Multiply by
35mm footage	16mm footage	$^2/_5$ or .4
35mm footage	Seconds	$^2/_3$ or .667
35mm footage	Frames	16
16mm footage	35mm footage	$2^1/_2$ or 2.5
16mm footage	Seconds	$1^2/_3$ or 1.667
16mm footage	Frames	40
Seconds	16mm footage	$^3/_5$ or .6
Seconds	35mm footage	$1^1/_2$ or 1.5
Seconds	Frames	24
Frames	16mm footage	$^1/_{40}$ or .025
Frames	35mm footage	$^1/_{16}$ or .0625
Frames	Seconds	$^1/_{24}$ or .04167

Equivalent Frame Clicks and Metronome Beats

Frame Click Beat	Metronome Beat*	Frame Click Beat	Metronome Beat*
8	180	16	90
8/2	174½	16/2	88½
8/4	169½	16/4	87½
8/6	164½	16/6	86
9	160	17	85
9/2	155½	17/2	83½
9/4	151½	17/4	82½
9/6	147½	17/6	81
10	144	18	80
10/2	140½	18/2	79
10/4	137	18/4	78
10/6	134	18/6	77
11	131	19	76
11/2	128	19/2	75
11/4	125	19/4	74
11/6	122½	19/6	73
12	120	20	72
12/2	117½	20/2	71
12/4	115	20/4	70
12/6	113	20/6	69½
13	111	21	68½
13/2	108½	21/2	68
13/4	106½	21/4	67
13/6	105	21/6	66
14	103	22	65½
14/2	101	22/2	64½
14/4	99½	22/4	64
14/6	97½	22/6	63½
15	96	23	62½
15/2	94½	23/2	62
15/4	93	23/4	61½
15/6	91½	23/6	60½
		24	60

*Metronome beats are computed to the nearest half.

Equivalent Footage and Seconds

Feet	Seconds		Feet	Seconds
1 =	0:00⅔		39 =	0:26
2 =	0:01⅓		40 =	0:26⅔
3 =	0:02		41 =	0:27⅓
4 =	0:02⅔		42 =	0:28
5 =	0:03⅓		43 =	0:28⅔
6 =	0:04		44 =	0:29⅓
7 =	0:04⅔		45 =	0:30
8 =	0:05⅓			
9 =	0:06		46 =	0:30⅔
10 =	0:06⅔		47 =	0:31⅓
11 =	0:07⅓		48 =	0:32
12 =	0:08		49 =	0:32⅔
13 =	0:08⅔		50 =	0:33⅓
14 =	0:09⅓		51 =	0:34
15 =	0:10		52 =	0:34⅔
16 =	0:10⅔		53 =	0:35⅓
17 =	0:11⅓		54 =	0:36
18 =	0:12		55 =	0:36⅔
19 =	0:12⅔		56 =	0:37⅓
20 =	0:13⅓		57 =	0:38
21 =	0:14		58 =	0:38⅔
22 =	0:14⅔		59 =	0:39⅓
23 =	0:15⅓		60 =	0:40
24 =	0:16			
25 =	0:16⅔		61 =	0:40⅔
26 =	0:17⅓		62 =	0:41⅓
27 =	0:18		63 =	0:42
28 =	0:18⅔		64 =	0:42⅔
29 =	0:19⅓		65 =	0:43⅓
30 =	0:20		66 =	0:44
			67 =	0:44⅔
31 =	0:20⅔		68 =	0:45⅓
32 =	0:21⅓		69 =	0:46
33 =	0:22		70 =	0:46⅔
34 =	0:22⅔		71 =	0:47⅓
35 =	0:23⅓		72 =	0:48
36 =	0:24		73 =	0:48⅔
37 =	0:24⅔		74 =	0:49⅓
38 =	0:25⅓		75 =	0:50

Equivalent Footage and Seconds (cont.)

Feet Seconds	*Feet Seconds*
76 = 0:50⅔	114 = 1:16
77 = 0:51⅓	115 = 1:16⅔
78 = 0:52	116 = 1:17⅓
79 = 0:52⅔	117 = 1:18
80 = 0:53⅓	118 = 1:18⅔
81 = 0:54	119 = 1:19⅓
82 = 0:54⅔	120 = 1:20
83 = 0:55⅓	
84 = 0:56	121 = 1:20⅔
85 = 0:56⅔	122 = 1:21⅓
86 = 0:57⅓	123 = 1:22
87 = 0:58	124 = 1:22⅔
88 = 0:58⅔	125 = 1:23⅓
89 = 0:59⅓	126 = 1:24
90 = 1:00	127 = 1:24⅔
91 = 1:00⅔	128 = 1:25⅓
92 = 1:01⅓	129 = 1:26
93 = 1:02	130 = 1:26⅔
94 = 1:02⅔	131 = 1:27⅓
95 = 1:03⅓	132 = 1:28
96 = 1:04	133 = 1:28⅔
97 = 1:04⅔	134 = 1:29⅓
98 = 1:05⅓	135 = 1:30
99 = 1:06	
100 = 1:06⅔	136 = 1:30⅔
101 = 1:07⅓	137 = 1:31⅓
102 = 1:08	138 = 1:32
103 = 1:08⅔	139 = 1:32⅔
104 = 1:09⅓	140 = 1:33⅓
105 = 1:10	141 = 1:34
	142 = 1:34⅔
106 = 1:10⅔	143 = 1:35⅓
107 = 1:11⅓	144 = 1:36
108 = 1:12	145 = 1:36⅔
109 = 1:12⅔	146 = 1:37⅓
110 = 1:13⅓	147 = 1:38
111 = 1:14	148 = 1:38⅔
112 = 1:14⅔	149 = 1:39⅓
113 = 1:15⅓	150 = 1:40

Feet	Seconds		Feet	Seconds
151	= 1:40⅔		191	= 2:07⅓
152	= 1:41⅓		192	= 2:08
153	= 1:42		193	= 2:08⅔
154	= 1:42⅔		194	= 2:09⅓
155	= 1:43⅓		195	= 2:10
156	= 1:44			
157	= 1:44⅔		196	= 2:10⅔
158	= 1:45⅓		197	= 2:11⅓
159	= 1:46		198	= 2:12
160	= 1:46⅔		199	= 2:12⅔
161	= 1:47⅓		200	= 2:13⅓
162	= 1:48		201	= 2:14
163	= 1:48⅔		202	= 2:14⅔
164	= 1:49⅓		203	= 2:15⅓
165	= 1:50		204	= 2:16
			205	= 2:16⅔
166	= 1:50⅔		206	= 2:17⅓
167	= 1:51⅓		207	= 2:18
168	= 1:52		208	= 2:18⅔
169	= 1:52⅔		219	= 2:19⅓
170	= 1:53⅓		210	= 2:20
171	= 1:54			
172	= 1:54⅔		211	= 2:20⅔
173	= 1:55⅓		212	= 2:21⅓
174	= 1:56		213	= 2:22
175	= 1:56⅔		214	= 2:22⅔
176	= 1:57⅓		215	= 2:23⅓
177	= 1:58		216	= 2:24
178	= 1:58⅔		217	= 2:24⅔
179	= 1:59⅓		218	= 2:25⅓
180	= 2:00		219	= 2:26
			220	= 2:26⅔
181	= 2:00⅔		221	= 2:27⅓
182	= 2:01⅓		222	= 2:28
183	= 2:02		223	= 2:28⅔
184	= 2:02⅔		224	= 2:29⅓
185	= 2:03⅓		225	= 2:30
186	= 2:04			
187	= 2:04⅔		226	= 2:30⅔
188	= 2:05⅓		227	= 2:31⅓
189	= 2:06		228	= 2:32
190	= 2:06⅔		229	= 2:32⅔

Equivalent Footage and Seconds (cont.)

Feet	Seconds	Feet	Seconds
230 =	2:33⅓	268 =	2:58⅔
231 =	2:34	269 =	2:59⅓
232 =	2:34⅔	270 =	3:00
233 =	2:35⅓	271 =	3:00⅔
234 =	2:36	272 =	3:01⅓
235 =	2:36⅔	273 =	3:02
236 =	2:37⅓	274 =	3:02⅔
237 =	2:38	275 =	3:03⅓
238 =	2:38⅔	276 =	3:04
239 =	2:39⅓	277 =	3:04⅔
240 =	2:40	278 =	3:05⅓
241 =	2:40⅔	279 =	3:06
242 =	2:41⅓	280 =	3:06⅔
243 =	2:42	281 =	3:07⅓
244 =	2:42⅔	282 =	3:08
245 =	2:43⅓	283 =	3:08⅔
246 =	2:44	284 =	3:09⅓
247 =	2:44⅔	285 =	3:10
248 =	2:45⅓	286 =	3:10⅔
249 =	2:46	287 =	3:11⅓
250 =	2:46⅔	288 =	3:12
251 =	2:47⅓	289 =	3:12⅔
252 =	2:48	290 =	3:13⅓
253 =	2:48⅔	291 =	3:14
254 =	2:49⅓	292 =	3:14⅔
255 =	2:50	293 =	3:15⅓
256 =	2:50⅔	294 =	3:16
257 =	2:51⅓	295 =	3:16⅔
258 =	2:52	296 =	3:17⅓
259 =	2:52⅔	297 =	3:18
260 =	2:53⅓	298 =	3:18⅔
261 =	2:54	299 =	3:19⅓
262 =	2:54⅔	300 =	3:20
263 =	2:55⅓	301 =	3:20⅔
264 =	2:56	302 =	3:21⅓
265 =	2:56⅔	303 =	3:22
266 =	2:57⅓	304 =	3:22⅔
267 =	2:58	305 =	3:23⅓

Feet	Seconds		Feet	Seconds
306	3:24		346	3:50⅔
307	3:24⅔		347	3:51⅓
308	3:25⅓		348	3:52
309	3:26		349	3:52⅔
310	3:26⅔		350	3:53⅓
311	3:27⅓		351	3:54
312	3:28		352	3:54⅔
313	3:28⅔		353	3:55⅓
314	3:29⅓		354	3:56
315	3:30		355	3:56⅔
316	3:30⅔		356	3:57⅓
317	3:31⅓		357	3:58
318	3:32		358	3:58⅔
319	3:32⅔		359	3:59⅓
320	3:33⅓		360	4:00
321	3:34		361	4:00⅔
322	3:34⅔		362	4:01⅓
323	3:35⅓		363	4:02
324	3:36		364	4:02⅔
325	3:36⅔		365	4:03⅓
326	3:37⅓		366	4:04
327	3:38		367	4:04⅔
328	3:38⅔		368	4:05⅓
329	3:39⅓		369	4:06
330	3:40		370	4:06⅔
331	3:40⅔		371	4:07⅓
332	3:41⅓		372	4:08
333	3:42		373	4:08⅔
334	3:42⅔		374	4:09⅓
335	3:43⅓		375	4:10
336	3:44		376	4:10⅔
337	3:44⅔		377	4:11⅓
338	3:45⅓		378	4:12
339	3:46		379	4:12⅔
340	3:46⅔		380	4:13⅓
341	3:47⅓		381	4:14
342	3:48		382	4:14⅔
343	3:48⅔		383	4:15⅓
344	3:49⅓		384	4:16
345	3:50		385	4:16⅔

Equivalent Footage and Seconds (cont.)

Feet	*Seconds*	*feet*	*Seconds*
386	= 4:17⅓	419	= 4:39⅓
387	= 4:18	420	= 4:40
388	= 4:18⅔	421	= 4:40⅔
389	= 4:19⅓	422	= 4:41⅓
390	= 4:20	423	= 4:42
391	= 4:20⅔	424	= 4:42⅔
392	= 4:21⅓	425	= 4:43⅓
393	= 4:22	426	= 4:44
394	= 4:22⅔	427	= 4:44⅔
395	= 4:23⅓	428	= 4:45⅓
396	= 4:24	429	= 4:46
397	= 4:24⅔	430	= 4:46⅔
398	= 4:25⅓	431	= 4:47⅓
399	= 4:26	432	= 4:48
400	= 4:26⅔	433	= 4:48⅔
401	= 4:27⅓	434	= 4:49⅓
402	= 4:28	435	= 4:50
403	= 4:28⅔	436	= 4:50⅔
404	= 4:29⅓	437	= 4:51⅓
405	= 4:30	438	= 4:52
406	= 4:30⅔	439	= 4:52⅔
407	= 4:31⅔	440	= 4:53⅓
408	= 4:32	441	= 4:54
409	= 4:32⅔	442	= 4:54⅔
410	= 4:33⅓	443	= 4:55⅓
411	= 4:34	444	= 4:56
412	= 4:34⅔	445	= 4:56⅔
413	= 4:35⅓	446	= 4:57⅓
414	= 4:36	447	= 4:58
415	= 4:36⅔	448	= 4:58⅔
416	= 4:37⅓	449	= 4:59⅓
417	= 4:38	450	= 5:00
418	= 4:38⅔		

Cycles per Second for Each Note of the Piano Keyboard

C	4186.0091	G♯	415.3047
B	3951.0665	G	391.9954
A♯	3729.3101	F♯	369.9944
A	**3520.0000**	F	349.2282
G♯	3322.4376	E	329.6276
G	3135.9635	D♯	311.1270
F♯	2959.9554	D	293.6648
F	2793.8259	C♯	277.1826
E	2637.0205	C	261.6256 (middle C)
D♯	2489.0159	B	246.9416
D	2349.3182	A♯	233.0819
C♯	2217.4611	**A**	**220.0000**
C	2093.0045	G♯	207.6523
B	1975.5332	G	195.9977
A♯	1864.6551	F♯	184.9972
A	**1760.0000**	F	174.6141
G♯	1661.2188	E	164.8138
G	1567.9818	D♯	155.5635
F♯	1479.9777	D	146.8324
F	1396.9129	C♯	138.5913
E	1318.5102	C	130.8128
D♯	1244.5079	B	123.4708
D	1174.6591	A♯	116.5409
C♯	1108.7305	**A**	**110.0000**
C	1046.5022	G♯	103.8261
B	987.7666	G	97.9988
A♯	932.3275	F♯	92.4986
A	**880.0000**	F	87.3070
G♯	830.6094	E	82.4069
G	783.9909	D♯	77.7817
F♯	739.9888	D	73.4162
F	698.4565	C♯	69.2956
E	659.2551	C	65.4064
D♯	622.2540	B	61.7354
D	587.3295	A♯	58.2704
C♯	554.3653	**A**	**55.0000**
C	523.2511	G♯	51.9130
B	493.8833	G	48.9994
A♯	466.1638	F♯	46.2493
A	**440.0000**	F	43.6535

Cycles per Second for Each Note of the
Piano Keyboard (cont.)

E	41.2034	C	32.7032
D♯	38.8908	B	30.8677
D	36.7081	A♯	29.1352
C♯	34.6478	**A**	**27.5000**

Quick Reference Chart for Timing Four Bars of Music in Seconds

	Seconds for 4 Bars	
Click Tempo	4/4 Time	3/4 Time
7	4⅔	3½
7/4	5	3¾
8	5⅓	4
8/4	5⅔	4¼
9	6	4½
9/4	6⅓	4¾
10	6⅔	5
10/4	7	5¼
11	7⅓	5½
11/4	7⅔	5¾
12	8	6
12/4	8⅓	6¼
13	8⅔	6½
13/4	9	6¾
14	9⅓	7
14/4	9⅔	7¼
15	10	7½
15/4	10⅓	7¾
16	10⅔	8
16/4	11	8¼
17	11⅓	8½
17/4	11⅔	8¾
18	12	9
18/4	12⅓	9¼
19	12⅔	9½
19/4	13	9¾
20	13⅓	10
20/4	13⅔	10¼
21	14	10½
21/4	14⅓	10¾
22	14⅔	11
22/4	15	11¼
23	15⅓	11½
23/4	15⅔	11¾
24	16	12
24/4	16⅓	12¼
25	16⅔	12½
25/4	17	12¾
26	17⅓	13

How to Lengthen a Sustained Chord

Lengthening a sustained chord is a little tricky and cannot be done with a three-channel music track. It must be done either with a composite single stripe or with a left channel only.

Assume you have a long sustained chord or a sustained note that you need to stretch even longer. As long as it is sustained and there is no motion in it, it can be done.

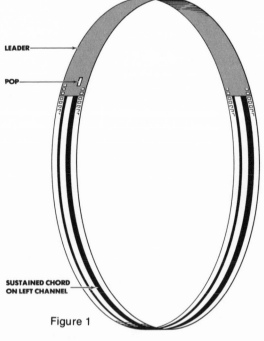

First: Remove the entire chord, or even a bit more, from the music track. It is just going to be borrowed and will be put back.

Loop it with a small piece of leader in between. Put a sync pop anywhere in the leader a few frames before the track comes in.

Note that the drawings are shown with the *magnetic side up,* making the left channel on the right side. See Figure 1.

LEADER

POP

SUSTAINED CHORD
ON LEFT CHANNEL

Figure 1

Second: Make about a half dozen copies, depending on how much you intend to stretch the chord. Transfer the loop to *both* the left and right channels of full-coat or three-channel stock. You can transfer it to all three but the center channel will not be needed. See Figure 2.

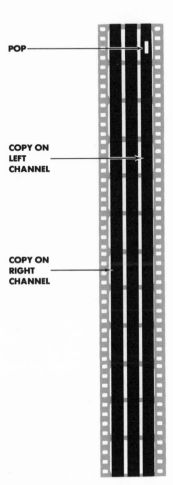

POP

COPY ON LEFT CHANNEL

COPY ON RIGHT CHANNEL

Figure 2

Third: On the synchronizer, line up the pops of all the copies *and the loop.* Put splice marks X and Y on all copies *and the loop.* These splice marks can be anywhere, as long as the sustained note is in progress between these two points. The further you can separate them, the fewer prints you will need because all you will be using on each print is what is between these marks. You can now open the loop and return it to the music track it came from. The X and Y are also marked on this loop. See Figure 3.

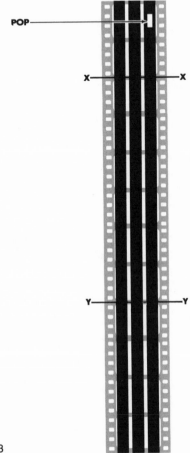

Figure 3

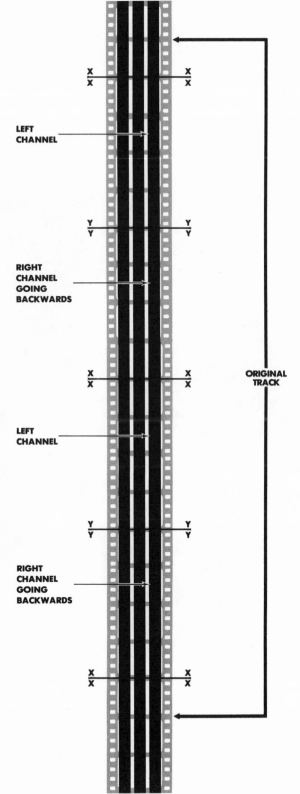

Fourth: As shown, splice copies for as long as you need, reversing each alternate copy. Each reversed copy is going backwards, but at each splice the modulations are identical. As long as the note is sustained, it will sound the same in either direction and there will be no change in dynamics.

This unit can now be cut into the original track which is also marked with an X and Y. If you want to shorten the new lengthened chord after putting it all together, you can remove identical amounts from both sides of *any* splice. The modulations will still match no matter how much you remove. See Figure 4.

LEFT CHANNEL

RIGHT CHANNEL GOING BACKWARDS

LEFT CHANNEL

RIGHT CHANNEL GOING BACKWARDS

ORIGINAL TRACK

Figure 4

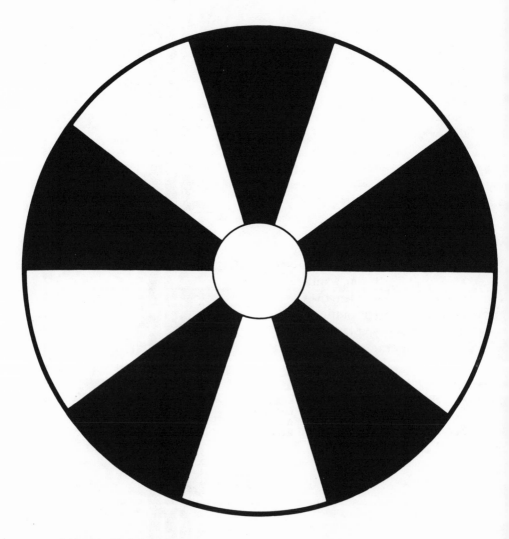

A Moviola Stroboscope

Glossary

Definitions given here apply to the words as they appear in this book and as they are used in the motion-picture industry. *Italic* type signifies a defined word or expression.

A reel, B reel—Theatrical release prints are mounted on 2000-foot reels. Work prints are on 1000-foot reels for convenience. All odd-numbered work reels are A reels; all even-numbered work reels are B reels. An A reel and a B reel thus make one theater reel. Hence the machine changeover (see *projection crossover*) in the projection room takes place only from a B reel to an A reel.

Academy leader—The standard *head leader* of a reel of film on which the start is exactly 12 feet from the first frame of picture. The leader is numbered on every foot.

Action—(1) An expression used to describe the reel of picture as opposed to the reel of sound. It may be referred to, for instance, as "reel 7 action." (2) "Action" is also used by the director while shooting as a signal for the actors to go into their performance.

ADR = Automatic Dialogue Replacement—A special process and a special studio designed for putting other dialogue on the film without physically taking the film apart to *loop* individual sequences.

Automatic dialogue replacement—See *ADR*.

Background noise—The sounds behind a recording.

Balance—The comparison between the different volume levels of different recorded sounds, for instance, the *balance* between the strings and the woodwinds.

Balance stripe—A narrow band of magnetic coating on 35mm stock. It lies in the position of the *right channel* and is not for recording; it gives the stock equal thickness along both the left and right channels and keeps it running straight.

Bar chart—A breakdown of the action of a scene put on music paper and indicating the actions in the form of music notations. See p. 89.

Bench—See *cutting bench*.

Bird's eye—A slang expression in music for a fermata (sustained note or chord). So called because its symbol ⌒ resembles an eye.

Break down—(1) To disassemble a roll of picture or sound track into all of its individual *takes*, both the good ones and the bad ones. (2) See *music breakdown*.

Channel—(1) A single *stripe* or *sound track* in a *three track* or *sixteen track*. (2) Also used as a verb; thus: "The dubbing mixer could channel the sound to record on another machine."

Click—See *What Is a Click?*, p. 42.

Click frame beat—Click tempo; see *click tempo*.

Click loops—See *Making a Set of Click Loops*, p. 46.

Click tempo—The specific tempo of a series of clicks, expressed as the number of frames and eighths of a frame between clicks.

Coded stripe—A magnetic track on stock that has only a single *stripe* on it and that has progressive numbers imprinted on it with a coding machine. See *The Coding Machine*, p. 72.

Coding—Imprinting numbers on a picture or sound track. These numbers advance automatically as the film goes through the *coding machine*.

Coding machine—A machine for *coding* film. See p. 72.

Composite single stripe—One *stripe* that carries the entire recording of the music of the film, as opposed to having the orchestra recording split up on various *channels* each of which carries a different section of the orchestra. Also called *monaural*.

Core—One of several words used for the plastic spool on which is wound a roll of film that is not on a reel. Also called a *hub*.

Critical synchronization—When *synchronizing* a picture and a sound track, an adjustment may be made by the shifting of one or more frames of either. When synchronizing two or more sound tracks, a shift of one or two *sprocket* holes may be called for; this adjustment is a critical synchronization.

Cue—A piece of music that plays with a scene is called a *cue*. During a *spotting* session, choosing points for starting or stopping the music is called *cueing*. Each cue is given an identifying number.

Cut—A change of scene, as in *cutting* from one scene to another.

Cutting bench—The editing table equipped with rewinds, *synchronizer*, and other items necessary for editing.

Cycle—Alternating current goes from zero to maximum in one direction, then to zero, then to maximum in the opposite direction, and back to zero. This sequence of events is called a *cycle*; in 60-cycle alternating current it takes place 60 times per second. Sound and music are similarly characterized by cycles; the number of cycles per second determines *pitch*.

Dailies—At the end of each day's work, all the sound and picture *takes* that were recorded and photographed that day comprise the *dailies*. For selection purposes, they are usually run in the order in which they were shot.

Daily code—A number code that is put on the *dailies* with the *coding machine*. This code will forever identify the scenes coded by these numbers. This code enables the sound track and picture track to be *synchronized*.

DBX—A noise-reduction process used in recording. It is different from *Dolby*.

Decoding—When, in reproducing an *encoded* recording, the *signal* is altered and restored to its original form but retains the reduction of noise, the process is called *decoding*.

Degauss—to completely remove all recorded sound from a magnetic sound track by passing the track through an alternating current.

Dialogue track—A sound track containing the dialogue of the picture it accompanies.

Digital control—The name for a special piece of equipment; see p. 44.

Digital delay—A special piece of equipment that can do unusual feats with sound, such as changing the pitch of music without changing the length or vice versa. The digital delay can also be used for echo and repeater effects.

Digital metronome—An electronic metronome that can be set to click the tempos of film beats in frames plus eighths of a frame.

Direct recording—See *playback*.

Dissolve—An overlapping fade-out of one scene with a fade-in of another scene. Also called a cross dissolve. Unlike a scene *cut*, which is abrupt, a dissolve is gradual.

Dolby—A noise-reduction process used in recording. It is different from *DBX*.

Dolly—(1) A wheeled platform for a camera, which can be easily moved toward or away from the subject. (2) To move the camera as on a dolly. *Dolly in* or *dolly back* indicates that the movement brings the camera closer to or further from the subject.

Downbeat—The first beat of a bar of music. The term is also used, incorrectly, to mean the start of a piece of music, which might in fact be on an upbeat.

Dub—(1) The process of combining all sound tracks into one single unit to run with the picture is called *dubbing*. (2) The combined track prepared on the *dubbing stage*.

Dubdown—A combination of a multichannel recording onto fewer channels than were originally recorded. A sixteen track might be dubbed down to a three track, or even to a single channel.

Dubbed master—The final *dubbed* product of a sound track, usually on three *stripes* of one piece of 35mm film. One stripe has music, one stripe has sound effects, and one stripe has dialogue/narration.

Dubbing console—A huge panel of controls in a dubbing room, through which all music, sound effects, and voice tracks must pass. Engineers control the volume settings and many other functions with the aid of very elaborate devices built into this console. The final *dub* is produced with this console.

Dubbing log—a *log* that accompanies the tracks, showing all the information needed for dubbing.

Dubbing mixer—An engineer who sits at a console and has control of all sound during dubbing. It is his product that is heard in the final version.

Dubbing stage—A small theater-like room equipped with seats and a *dubbing console,* behind which sit engineers who combine all the sounds and music from many tracks to achieve a final acceptable product.

Dubbing units—The individual rolls of sound recordings, whether music, sound effects, or voices, that will be sent to the *dubbing stage* for final dubbing.

Dupe—A copy of the original picture, whether in black-and-white or in color. It is used for work purposes by sound-effects editors, music editors, or loop editors. A duplicate.

Echo chamber—(1) A room that causes sounds to reverberate. (2) An electronic device that produces a similar effect.

Edit—(1) To *edit* a piece of music means to alter it either by removing a phrase or by lengthening it. Anything done to the music other than leaving it intact is considered editing. (2) An *edit* is a piece that has been edited or is to be edited.

Emulsion—The coating on the film which is the material sensitized for photography. If scraped off, it leaves the film clear.

Encoding—The process of altering a *signal* with any noise reduction system so that when it is subsequently *decoded* a reduction of noise occurs.

End leader—A piece of *leader* attached at the end of a reel to protect the end of the film, whether picture or sound. It also allows the film to run to its end without running out of the equipment and necessitating rethreading.

Engineer—See *recording engineer.*

EOL = end of line—One of many ways used to indicate the end of a bit of spoken word or dialogue in a timing sheet. It is used by some music editors. See page 37.

Equalization—altering the sound of a track with an *equalizer.*

Equalizer—An electronic device that can alter the sound of any recording channeled through it, by varying the amplitude of various frequencies.

Ex-copy—One of several expressions used in connection with *dubbing* when a *dubbed master* is transferred to another new master while making dubbing changes.

False start—When making a recording it is possible that after the first bar the take becomes no good. The recording is then started again; the preceding start is a *false start.* A log on the box containing the recording might say: "Take 1 HOLD / Take 2 FS / Take 3 OK." "FS" means *false start.*

Fermata—A musical expression. It is a direction to hold an indicated note or chord for an unspecified time until terminated by the conductor. The indicating symbol is also called a *fermata* or, colloquially, a *bird's eye* because of its appearance (⌒).

Fill—Another word for *leader*.

Film editor—The person who edits a picture from the *dailies* to the final stage.

Flange—A piece of editing-room equipment used for winding film without a reel. It is circular and flat and has a hub over which a core can be placed as the film is wound onto it. When the roll of film is removed it holds its shape without need of a reel.

Flat—(1) The *flat* is a musical notation indicating that a note's *pitch* is to be lowered one *half tone*. (2) A tone is *flat* if its pitch is lower than standard. (3) A note of correct pitch is said to be a *flat* when it is a half tone lower than the *natural* tone. Thus "E flat" or "B flat" is a half tone lower than "E natural" or "B natural."

Flatbed—A film-editing machine such as the KEM through which the film travels horizontally, in contrast to a Moviola in which the film's travel is vertical. The KEM is illustrated on p. 23.

Flopping—Turning a piece of sound track upside down before splicing it to another piece, thereby making the left channel of sound appear on the right side so as not to be capable of reproducing on a single-stripe head.

Flutter punch—A series of holes punched in alternate frames of the picture. See *The Newman System*, pp. 107–114.

Footage—The measurement of film in feet rather than in time units.

Footage counter—A counting machine that measures the *footage* of film. See the illustration, p. 24.

Frame—A single picture on the film. There are 16 frames to each foot of 35mm film. In referring to sound, one frame is equivalent to four *sprocket* holes.

Frame line—The line that separates each frame of film from its adjacent frame.

Free clicks—*Warning clicks,* which see.

Free timing—The manner in which a piece of music is played freely, not controlled by a rigid click tempo.

Frequency—The number of *cycles* per second. The frequency of an alternating-current power supply is 60 cycles per second, or 60 *hertz*. The *pitch* of a musical tone is established by the frequency of its sound; thus the note A above middle C has a frequency of 440 cycles per second or 440 hertz. Increasing or decreasing such a frequency raises or lowers the pitch correspondingly.

Frequency response—The range of *frequencies* that sound recording or reproducing equipment will record or reproduce faithfully. It is designated in hertz or in cycles per second, as 20–20,000 cycles per second or 20–20,000 hertz.

Full coat—Film *stock* which is completely covered with a magnetic coating; or, the coating on such film. This contrasts with transparent stock having individual *stripes* of coating.

Futz—To compress the high and low frequencies of sound, speech, or music.

In most telephones, in old radios or small transistor radios, and in inferior sound equipment the signal becomes *futzed;* in motion pictures, sound is futzed to give the impression that it comes over the small speakers of such equipment.

Guide track—A *sound track* usually listened to on earphones while recording. A vocalist replacing another vocalist would listen to the old track and follow it.

Half tone—The tonal distance between any note and its adjacent higher or lower note. From G to G sharp is a half tone, also from G to G flat.

Head—(1) The beginning of a reel of film or tape is called the *head* of the reel. (2) The magnetic reproducer or recorder over which film or tape passes; see *sound head.*

Hertz—A unit of frequency, one *cycle* per second.

Hiss—A common expression for *background noise.*

Hub—See *core.*

In the open—Music that is heard without interfering or accompanying sound effects or voices is said to play *in the open.*

Input—An audio signal going into a reproducer or recorder is being fed into the *input* of the equipment. The signal thus fed may also be called the *input.* The amplified or altered signal that comes out is called the *output.*

Intercut—Cutting together different portions of different takes is called *intercutting.*

Interlock—To run two or more recorders or reproducers together so that they are *synchronized.*

Interval—The tonal distance between any two notes of music is an *interval.*

Leader—Old picture *stock* used for building units for dubbing. Also called *fill* or *spacer.* Any piece of film can be called leader when it has no significant purpose other than to keep sections of sound track in *synchronization.*

Left channel—On 35mm sound stock, the *left channel* is on the left when the magnetic side is down and the track is traveling away from the observer or operator. This channel is called the left channel even if the stock is *flopped* or turned.

Line scriber—A piece of equipment used to scribe visual lines on the film for the *scoring stage.* Also called a *streamer board.* It is described on pages 98–101.

Log—Any kind of chart prepared for a special purpose, as a *dubbing log,* a *recording stage log,* or other.

Looping—(1) Making a loop of any sound track or picture so that it can be run repeatedly. (2) The rerecording of new lines of dialogue to replace old ones, even though the change is not actually done by looping.

Magnetic sound reproduction—A method of sound reproduction by means of a piece of film or tape that has a magnetic coating which when passed over a magnetic *head* converts the *modulations* to sound.

Millisecond—One one-thousandth of a second (.001 sec.).

Minus dialogue—One of several expressions that indicate a *dubbed* sound track with music and sound effects but with no dialogue or narration. Such track is used for dubbing in a foreign language together with the new translated track.

Mixer—(1) Same as *dubbing mixer*. (2) A piece of electronic equipment that can combine many *signal inputs* and *channel* them to a single *output*.

Modulation—When a *magnetic track* has a recorded sound of any kind on it, it is said to be *modulated*.

Monaural—See *composite single stripe*.

Moviola—The name of a patented film-editing machine, the one currently in widest use. See the illustration, p. 22.

Music breakdown—The information supplied to the music editor, resulting from a *spotting* session. The breakdown indicates the starts and stops of the music cues decided upon, all of which have been given cue numbers.

Music code—A code put on the film with the *coding machine* and used for *synchronizing*. Different numbers and letters prevent any confusion between this code and the *daily code*.

Music continuity—The listing of all music cues in sequential order.

Music editor—One who edits music for motion pictures.

Music recording session—A recording session in which the music for a motion picture is recorded.

Natural—The tone produced by any of the white keys on a piano keyboard, as "A natural." See also *flat, sharp*.

Noise-reduction system—An electronic system that helps reduce the amount of *background noise* in a recording, hence improves the *signal-to-noise ratio*. Dolby and DBX are two such systems.

Nonvisual source music—*Source music* that is heard, but not seen in the film, for example a radio. An on-screen vocalist would be visual source.

One to one—A copy of a sound track recorded at the same volume as the one from which it is reproduced, so that the copy is identical.

Optical sound reproduction—The method of sound reproduction accomplished by a fluctuating light that passes over a photoelectric cell. It is in use today for theater-release prints. The sound track to the left of the picture on a theater-release print is an optical track; this is not visible on the screen.

Orchestra chart—A chart showing the instrument breakdown of each music cue to be played at a recording session.

Output—The *output* of an amplifier is the element that connects to the speaker or to the *input* of other electronic equipment.

Overtones—(1) The decaying sound after the initial attack of a musical note or chord. (2) A component of a higher frequency of the fundamental tone.

Pan—A camera movement, as in "pan to the left," "pan upwards," or the like.

Pickup—(1) A piece of music starting before the downbeat of a bar; it might be only one or two notes. (2) To *pick up* a sound means to record it. (3) If a cue is being recorded and it goes bad near the end, the conductor—rather than start again from the beginning—may say, "Let's make a *pickup* from bar 30 to the end."

Picture editor—Same as *film editor*.

Pitch—The tonality of a note as related to the musical scale. Increasing the *frequency* raises the pitch; lowering the frequency lowers the pitch.

Pitch changer—Equipment that can lower the *pitch* of music electronically. Pitch can also be changed by changing the speed of the reproducer.

Playback—A recording of any kind that will be used for photography later, with the actors mouthing or dancing to the playback track that they hear. By contrast, in a *direct recording*, the recording and the photography are done simultaneously.

Playback head—The magnetic *head* that receives a *signal* from a tape or track and converts it into sound or music. See also *sound head*.

Playback machine—A tape player or record player that plays the *playback* on the set for photography.

Playback recording session—The music *recording session* at which music is recorded only for the *playbacks*. This is done before any photography, as opposed to the recording session for the *scoring*.

Pop—A loud high-pitched sound of very short duration, used for synchronization purposes. See also *tone beep, sync pop*.

Prescoring—Another name for the *playback recording*.

Production track—A sound track recorded simultaneously with the photography.

Projection crossover—Making the change at the end of a reel to the next reel on another projection machine. This requires critical timing, which is done by the projectionist with the aid of inconspicuous markings on the film.

Prologue—A short recapitulation of what has happened previously. This is placed on the *timing sheets* as explained in the text. See pp. 36–37.

Public domain—The status of music or story material which is not owned or controlled by any owner, that is, which is not protected by copyright. It may be of unknown origin, or if of known origin, may have come into the public domain by the passage of time. Music and other material of known origin comes into the public domain after a specified date, but this date must be determined for each individual composition.

Pull-up—A short copied section from the *dub* at the *head* of a reel, put at the end of the outgoing reel for laboratory purposes.

Punch—See *flutter punch* and *The Newman System*, pp. 107–114.

Quarter tone—The tonality midway between any note and the adjacent note that is a *half tone* higher or lower.

Recording engineer—The engineer who sits at the console and *balances* the music as he records it. See also *recordist.*

Recordist—The person who operates the equipment on which the recording is made; not to be confused with the *recording engineer,* who sits at the console.

Resolver—A piece of electronic equipment that controls the *frequency* of the electric current; it can be used to change the frequency. A resolver also controls the playing of a recorded track on tape at the precise speed at which it was recorded; thus it acts as a governor.

Reverberation chamber—Same as *echo chamber.*

Rheostat—A control used to increase or decrease the flow of electric current by varying the resistance.

Right channel—See the explanation of *left channel;* the right channel is the one on the opposite side of the stock.

Ritard—A musical direction meaning to slow down gradually.

Scoring—(1) The music scored for the picture. This term differentiates between *scoring* and *source music.* See p. 27. (2) The *recording session.*

Scoring log—A *log* set up for the recording session. See the illustration, p. 103.

Scoring session—The *recording session.*

Scoring stage—A recording stage that is set up to score a film. It has projection, a *stop clock,* and a *digital metronome* in addition to other equipment.

Scribing tool—A tool used for scribing the emulsion when making *streamers* on a *line scriber.* It is usually a pin punch, and can be purchased wherever tools are sold.

Seconds counter—A counting machine for timing a film in seconds. See the illustration, p. 24.

Segue (pronounced *seg-way*)—A musical expression meaning to go from one piece of music to another without stopping.

Set—The shooting stage on which the photography is done.

Set horn—A loudspeaker used on a *set* to play *guide tracks* or *playbacks* for the actors.

Set track—A *sound track* that is recorded while shooting, and thus while hearing the *playback.* It is a rerecording of the playback and the sound is of poor quality. It is used as a guide for cutting the final track.

Sharp—(1) The *sharp* is a musical notation indicating that *pitch* is to be raised one *half tone.* (2) A tone is *sharp* if its pitch is higher than standard. (3) A note of correct pitch is called a *sharp* when it is a half tone higher than the *natural* tone. Thus "G sharp" or "A sharp" is a half tone higher than "G natural" or "A natural."

Shoot—To do the photography for a film. Hence "the *shooting,*" "the film is being *shot.*"

Sideline musicians—Musicians who appear in a film and pretend to play. They may actually be playing, but their music is not being recorded. They follow a *playback* just as the actors do.

Signal—The sound from a track, tape, or record, or the modulated electric current that forms the sound. The signal that is fed into the *input* of any electronic equipment is called the input signal. A piece of film may be described as having no signal on it if it has been *degaussed* or has not been *modulated*.

Signal-to-noise ratio—The ratio of the volume of the recorded sound to the volume of the *background noise*. The greater or higher the signal-to-noise ratio, the better the quality. A very low signal-to-noise ratio means that it is difficult to separate the background noise from the recorded sound.

Single stripe—A 35mm sound track with a magnetic *stripe* on the *left channel* only. The rest of the film is clear except for the *balance stripe*.

16mm film—Film 16mm wide; standard motion-picture film is 35mm film. The 16mm film is much used in industrial and amateur movies. It has 40 frames per foot as opposed to 16 frames per foot for 35mm film, but both run at 24 frames per second sound speed.

Sixteen track—(1) A recording machine on which the recording, playback, and erase heads are each composed of sixteen individual adjacent heads. This equipment enables one to record sixteen different channels simultaneously on a tape 2 inches wide. Each channel is completely isolated. The machine also permits the same person to record on the sixteen channels, one at a time; all the channels can then be played back together. This practice is very much in use with small groups. (2) The expression *sixteen track* also refers to the tape.

Sketch—Music written by a composer and put down rather broadly on music paper is called a *sketch*. These sketches then go to the orchestrator; after orchestration, they are sent to the copyist. The music appearing in this book is in sketch form.

Slate—(1) On a sound track, a voice *signal* placed on it to identify the recording. (2) To place this voice signal, as in "*Slate* your tempos." See also *slate board*.

Slate board—A small hand-held blackboard with chalk-written identification of scene numbers, *take* numbers, and other pertinent data. It is held in front of the camera and photographed prior to the shooting; a hinged stick is closed quickly to make an audible signal. *Dailies* are synchronized by matching the visible closing of the stick with the sound made on the sound track.

Sound-effects editor—An editor who cuts the sound effects for a film is called a *sound-effects editor*. Much of what he does comes from a vast library of sound effects. If a needed effect is not available, the editor will record what is necessary and then cut it into his *dubbing units*.

Sound head—The *sound head* is the *head* over which tape or film passes for recording or reproducing. The recording takes place as the film or tape passes over a hardly visible gap in the *recording head*. This head, with the aid of a recording amplifier, aligns the molecules on the magnetic coating. Once this has been done, the material recorded on the tape can be eliminated only by erasing or *degaussing*. A *playback head* does not affect the molecular alignment.

Sound reader—A small piece of equipment used on an editing bench. It has a small amplifier and a sound reproducing head but no motor; film is pulled through it by hand. It is used to determine the exact point on the film for which one is looking. It is a convenience but very limited in its use.

Sound track—The magnetic or optical *stripe* on film *stock*, which is modulated in the process of recording music, dialogue, or other sound. It may be *full coat, stripe,* or *optical.*

Source music—See *Source Music and Scoring*, p. 27.

Spacer—See *leader.*

Split—To *split* a track means to put a portion of it on one unit and another portion on a different unit. The tracks must be in *sync* at the join of each so that when one unit has played its portion the next unit immediately takes over. A good reason for splitting a track is explained in the chapter *Editing Source Music,* pp. 129–132.

Spotting—Running a film to locate and indicate the various places for starting and stopping the music *cues.*

Sprockets—(1) The holes in the film which are used for transporting the film through all film equipment. (2) *Sprocket* can accordingly be used as a unit of measurement of sound duration, each sprocket indicating one quarter of a frame (¼ frame) in 35mm film, that is, $1/96$ second. (3) The teeth on any roller that pulls film are called *sprockets* or *sprocket teeth.*

Stage playback—See *playback.*

Start mark—A mark of any kind on the film to indicate where to thread up or where to measure from.

Sting—A slang musical expression meaning a strong chord hit to emphasize an action. Stings are used much more in television than in theater films.

Stock—The film material: sound stock, picture stock, and so on. A person ordering prints might be asked on what *stock* it should be recorded, as *full coat* or *stripe.*

Stopclock—A timepiece like a stopwatch except that it is larger, usually about 6 inches in diameter, sometimes more. It is set up to be seen by the conductor.

Stopwatch—See *The Stopwatch*, p. 28.

Streamer—A warning mark on film. (1) For use in *scoring*, it is a line that travels across the screen as a guide for the conductor to be prepared for an incoming *cue.* (2) For use on a dubbing stage, a streamer is a similar mark to indicate an upcoming action that must be executed.

Streamer board—The same as a *line scriber.* Its use and the method for making it is thoroughly explained on pp. 98–101.

Stripe—A ribbon of magnetic coating applied to a piece of film. The rest of the film is clear stock except for a balance stripe.

Stroboscope—A device for measuring the speed of a rotating object, typically a shaft or turntable. The device is a disk that rotates with the part; the observer's view is interrupted, usually by the normally unperceived variations in light from a 60-cycle alternating current. Marks on the moving device are thus seen only intermittently; they are spaced to make them seen at the same point in successive rotations, wherefore the rotating device appears to stand still when moving at the speed for which the marks are designed.

Sustain—To hold a note or chord for a period of time; the sound is thus a *sustained* note or chord. A *fermata* written above a note in the music sheet is a direction to sustain it.

Sweeten—To augment a piece of music that has been recorded, by adding music on top of it in order to enhance it. The added music is called a *sweetener.*

Sync *or* synchronization—"In sync" means that the sound is in correct synchronization with the picture—that it is heard at the exactly correct time, neither earlier nor later.

Synchronize *or* sync—To *synchronize* is to make two or more elements (as a picture and a sound track) run together with the corresponding details coinciding exactly.

Synchronizer—A piece of equipment used on a *cutting bench.* It allows for running several tracks or picture in *sync.* A photograph of a synchronizer appears on page 53.

Sync pop—A loud but very short sound inserted into a sound track for any of several purposes. It is *not* heard on the finished track. In *dubbing,* a sync pop may be cut into the sound track at a chosen point somewhere before the picture starts (which is at 12 feet); a corresponding mark is put on the picture. Using the sync pop and the mark, the laboratory can line up the recorded sound with the picture for processing. A sync pop can also be used when making transfers of a sound track; copies can then be lined up in sync simply by lining up the pops. An *end pop* is placed at a point after a reel ends. See also *tone beeps* and p. 80.

Sync pulse—This is explained in detail under the heading, p. 70.

Tail—The end of a reel, whether picture or track.

Take—A word used for identification purposes. A recording made for the first time is called *take one.* If the same recording is done a second time, it is called *take two.* The take number enables the editor to identify which recording is finally selected. The term *take* is not restricted to recordings; it is also used in referring to photography.

Takeup—A device used to take the film up as it is being run. Some editors have *takeup* arms on the Moviola, which wind the film on reels. (Other editors working on a Moviola may run the film into a basket.) The takeup arms are removable to suit the needs of the person operating the machine.

Tempo—Tempo refers to the interval between successive beats. A 12 beat is slower tempo than a 10 beat. Musical expressions indicating tempo are allegro, vivace, andante, and the like.

Theme—The melody or piece of music that identifies a particular person or incident. A love theme or a menace theme is identifying.

35mm film—The industry's standard width for professional motion-picture film is 35mm (very close to 1⅜ inches). There is also *16mm film,* and 8mm film, which is used for home movies.

Three channel, three track, three stripe—These expressions are used interchangeably and are substantially synonymous. See *channel, sound track, stripe.*

Time clock—See *stopclock.*

Time code—A series of numbers imprinted on a videocassette copy of a film. It is superimposed on top of the picture and indicates elapsed time. See p. 34.

Timing—Taking down the pictorial and audio continuity of a sequence for a composer is called *timing.* This is explained under *Timing on the Moviola,* p. 30.

Timing sheet—See *timing.*

Tone beep—A device used for applying *sync pops* to a track. Tone beeps are supplied on ¼-inch tape with a backing that allows a short piece to be peeled off and stuck onto a sound track. They have a signal recorded on them at about 1000 cycles, which produces a piercing sound. When tone beeps are not available, a single frame of 35mm can be used and cut into a sound track so long as it has the same piercing frequency on it.

Track—A *sound track.* Also see *channel, stripe.*

Tracking—To *track* means to edit music from a library for a picture. If the music were not recorded for the sequences but obtained from already-recorded material, it would be said that the sequences were *tracked.* Entire features can be and have been tracked from music libraries.

Transfer—To make a copy of a sound track from any medium to any medium, as film to tape, tape to film, cassette to film, or the like.

Tremolo—A musical expression. On bowed instruments it is the rapid reiteration of a note by up and down strokes. It is also the rapid alternation of two notes of an interval.

Triple head—This expression may refer to the magnetic *head* or to the film. (1) In reference to the magnetic recording or reproducing head it would mean three individual heads mounted adjacently for recording three separate channels of sound or three stripes of magnetic coating on the film. (2) *Triple head* may also refer to the piece of magnetic stock with three separate stripes of coating. A roll of *full coat* may also be called a *triple head* if it has three channels recorded on it.

Under the dialogue—Any sound, whether music or sound effects, which is played at low volume to allow the dialogue to be heard is said to be *under the dialogue.*

Unit—The individual roll of old picture *stock* into which *sound track* is edited in *sync* with the picture and used for *dubbing.*

Unmodulated—Magnetic track that has no sound on it, either because none has ever been recorded on it or because it has been *degaussed,* is said to be *unmodulated.*

Variable click track—A *click track* where the tempo is not identical between successive beats but varies according to what is required.

Videocassette—A cassette which when played on a video recorder produces the picture and the sound on a television screen.

Visual source music—*Source music* that can be seen in a picture, as when someone sings on camera. If the person were singing off camera or if the music were from a radio it would be source music but not visual.

Voice replacement—See *ADR.*

Warning clicks—The clicks heard before the start of music to give the tempo for the incoming music.

Wild—A *wild* recording is one that is made without any restricting tempo or clicks. If it is not recorded to a picture it may also be called *wild.*

Work copy, work picture, work print, work track—Any picture or track used just for work purposes. A *dupe* picture may be called a *work copy.* A *work track* is a copy made from an original track.

Index